INFORMATION
& FORMATION

ABOUT LANDSCAPE, ARCHITECTURE AND CITIES

ÜBER LANDSCHAFT, ARCHITEKTUR UND STÄDTE

LAAC

KATHRIN ASTE
& FRANK LUDIN

PARK BOOKS

There are many notions of which principles should be followed by architectural form. Form follows: function, fiction, fashion, vision, technology, motion, the golden section, the genius loci, the clients' ideas. All of these are relevant, but none exclusively so.

Our architectural practice of the past fifteen years has taught us that architecture is a subject that follows a complex cognitive process, which not so much defines a conclusive solution as formulates a synthesis that is constantly being reformulated on the basis of new parameters. This process oscillates between perception and design, between information and formation.

The partly intuitive and partly methodical process that shapes an architectural design is known as form-finding and form-giving. Form-finding describes a search that generates knowledge, which informs and thus establishes a form based on objective, functional and generally understood criteria, whereas form-giving denotes how we select and, thus, designate the shape of a building.

This catalogue employs a diverse range of realised buildings to illustrate the interaction between form-finding and form-giving, whose contributions to projects are dynamic and never linear. These range from the interaction with natural elements, via the transformation of urban and social spaces, to the impact of digital processes on architectural form. And even if form-finding is a predominantly analytical process and there is no predefined formal concept, we understand form-giving to be a creative, tectonic practice that establishes a relationship between society and the environment, between the functional and the possible.

Information & Formation reminds us that design, production and building are together acts of argumentation and debate that we perform, not to satisfy the demands of constructional functionalism and capitalistic investment logic, but in order to meet the challenges of today and tomorrow in a positively critical and aesthetically responsible way.

CONTENTS

VORWORT

Es gibt viele Vorstellungen davon, welchen Prinzipien die architektonische Form folgt. Form follows – function, fiction, fashion, vision, technology, motion, dem Goldenen Schnitt, dem Genius Loci, den Ideen der Bauherrin oder des Bauherrn. Alles davon ist relevant, nichts davon ausschließlich.

Die architektonische Praxis der letzten 15 Jahre hat uns gelehrt, dass Architektur eine Materie ist, die einem komplexen kognitiven Prozess folgt, der weniger eine endgültige Lösung definiert, als eine Synthese formuliert, die sich immer wieder auf Basis neuer Parameter konstituiert. Dieser Vorgang pendelt zwischen Erkenntnis und Gestaltung, zwischen Information und Formation.

Mit Formfindung und Formgebung werden dabei jene Prozesse beschrieben, die teils methodisch, teils intuitiv den architektonischen Entwurf prägen. Befinden wir uns im Zuge der Formfindung auf einer Suche, die uns Kenntnis verschafft, also informiert und dementsprechend die Form auf eine objektive funktionale allgemeinverständliche Basis stellt, interpretieren und selektieren wir in der Formgebung und erzeichnen dabei die Gestalt eines Bauwerks.

Dieser Katalog erzählt anhand diverser realisierter Bauwerke von der Wechselwirkung zwischen Formfindung und Formgebung, die aufregend und niemals linear die Projekte begleiten. Sie reichen von der Interaktion mit natürlichen Elementen über die Transformation urbaner und sozialer Räume bis hin zur Einflussnahme digitaler Prozesse auf die Form der Architektur. Auch wenn die Formfindung ein größtenteils analytischer Vorgang ist und es keine vordefinierte Formvorstellung gibt, so verstehen wir die Formgebung als künstlerische, tektonische Praxis, die Gesellschaft mit der Umwelt und das Funktionale mit dem Möglichen in Beziehung setzt.

Information & Formation erinnert uns, dass Entwerfen, Produzieren und Bauen ein Akt des Argumentierens und Debattierens sind, nicht um den Bauwirtschaftsfunktionalismus mit der kapitalistischen Investitionslogik zu verhandeln, sondern um in kritischer und freudiger Weise den gegenwärtigen und zukünftigen Herausforderungen in ästhetischer und sinnhafter Weise zu begegnen.

CONTENTS

STOP
POLIZEI
POLIZEI
HOTEL ROUTE
Hotel
Adlers

POLIZEI
HOT
SHOP

GAERTNER
BUS
BUS

READING THE LANDSCAPE

Kathrin Aste

It is only natural that the surroundings in which one grew up influence one's perception and how one reads and interprets one's environment. In our case, the powerfully shaped topography of the Alpine landscape, which is the result of a multitude of dynamic processes and events, plays a significant role in our sense of spatial awareness.

Parameters such as tectonics, formation, diversity and coexistence, which are borrowed from the landscape, are key aspects of our understanding of architecture. The compositional character of the landscape is our most important reference and our most powerful model for the design of the built environment.

In his book *The Sympathy of Things*, Lars Spuybroek writes that nature has an architectural tendency. He adds that there is a reason for the way that it is and refers to John Ruskin and his comparison of the landscape with a material index of forces, processes and relationships that unite to create a free characteristic form.[1] In our work, we echo the methods of cartography by creating digital drawings as a process of translation that reveals and illustrates the characteristics of a landscape. This process results in three-dimensional structures or patterns that affect the architectural design process in two ways. On the one hand, they enable us to draw conclusions about specific landscape situations by illustrating these and translating them into structures that, while abstract, are also highly informative. On the other hand, they typically function as patterns that generate formal models.[2] In this way, we establish a basis for our design that is rooted in a formal logic, which tells of events and relationships and which we ultimately perceive as beautiful.

Even if this process does not meet scientific standards and, as a result, the information that it generates has no universal validity, it still establishes structural principles that support and deepen our architectural ideas. In this sense, the understanding of nature illustrated by our drawings is less a numerically scientific than a pictorially artistic reading of the landscape. These structures contain information about the shape of landscape formations that includes their size, locational relationships, materiality, curvature and inclination as well as the topology of specific elements. They clarify the composition of the earth's surface, its grain, the local vegetation and how it is affected by cyclical phenomena such as the seasons, growth and erosion.

Levels of exposure and sunlight are further parameters that help us to understand the natural dynamic and the form and structure of the landscape. Other aspects that play a major role in determining the characteristics of the landscape include the difference between the short-range and long-range impact of both the landscape as a whole and its individual formal elements and the polarity between the inner terrain and the horizon.

Every architectural intervention is a visual description of a relationship with our environment that exists in contrast with natural conditions and cultural and technical reactions. The result is a multitude of built artefacts that recount the complex and challenging relationship between humans and nature. As a deeply anthropogenic discipline, architecture is particularly called upon to take its responsibility seriously and devote more attention to environmental issues. The depiction of the landscape helps us to understand that we are not building on a site but, rather, acting within a volume that consists of layers, organisms and closed loops. For us, architecture is much more than a figure in front of a background. Ideally, it is, like the landscape itself, a complex dynamic system and an adaptable sphere that remains open to transformation and development.

Natürlich beeinflusst die Umgebung, in der man aufgewachsen ist, die Wahrnehmung und wie man seine Umwelt liest und interpretiert. In unserem Falle dürfte die stark geformte Topografie der alpinen Landschaft, die aus einer Vielzahl dynamischer Prozesse und Ereignisse resultiert, eine maßgebliche Rolle für unsere Raumwahrnehmung spielen.

Aus der Landschaft entlehnte Parameter wie Tektonik, Formation, Diversität und Koexistenz sind wichtige Themen für unser Verständnis von Architektur. Die kompositorische Beschaffenheit der Landschaft ist unsere wichtigste Referenz und unser größtes Vorbild für den Entwurf der gebauten Umwelt.

„Die Natur hat eine architektonische Tendenz", schreibt Lars Spuybroek in dem Buch *The Sympathy of Things*. „Sie ist nicht ohne Grund so, wie sie ist." Er bezieht sich damit auf John Ruskin, der die Landschaft mit einem Materialindex aus Kräften, Prozessen und Beziehungen vergleicht, die sich zu einer freien charakteristischen Form vereinen.[1] Ähnlich der Kartografie erstellen wir digitale Zeichnungen als Übersetzungsverfahren, um die Eigenschaften einer Landschaft zu exponieren und zu visualisieren. Dabei entstehen dreidimensionale Strukturen bzw. Muster, die für den architektonischen Entwurfsprozess in zweierlei Hinsicht wirksam werden. Einerseits ermöglichen sie uns, Kenntnis über spezifische landschaftliche Situationen zu erlangen, indem wir diese sichtbar machen und in zwar abstrakte, aber aufschlussreiche Strukturen übersetzen; und andererseits fungieren sie bezeichnenderweise als Muster, die formale Vorbilder

1 Lars Spuybroek, *The Sympathy of Things: Ruskin and the Ecology of Design*, London 2011, S. 56.

2 Andrea Sick, *Kartenmuster. Bilder und Wissenschaft in der Kartografie*, Dissertation Universität Hamburg, 2002.

erstellen.[2] Wir schaffen uns damit eine Entwurfsgrundlage, die auf einer formalen Logik aufbaut, die von Ereignissen und Beziehungen erzählt, was wir schlussendlich als schön empfinden.

Auch wenn das Verfahren wissenschaftlichen Standards nicht standhält und dabei kein allgemeingültiges Wissen erzeugt wird, werden strukturelle Prinzipien extrahiert, die unsere architektonischen Ideen unterstützen und vertiefen. In diesem Sinne ist unser durch die Zeichnungen veranschaulichtes Naturverständnis weniger ein numerisch wissenschaftliches als ein bildhaft künstlerisches Lesen der Landschaft. Diese Strukturen beinhalten Informationen über die Gestalt landschaftlicher Formationen wie deren Größe, Lagebeziehung, Materialität, Krümmung, Neigung sowie die Topologie spezifischer Elemente. Sie verdeutlichen die Beschaffenheit der Erdoberfläche, ihre Körnung, die vorhandene Vegetation und wie sie sich im Kontext zyklischer Phänomene wie Jahreszeiten, Wachstum und Erosion verändert.

Exposition und Sonneneinstrahlung sind weitere Parameter, die relevant sind, um die natürliche Dynamik, die Form und die Struktur der Landschaft zu verstehen. Hinsichtlich der Charakteristik des Landschaftsbildes spielt auch der Unterschied zwischen Nah- und Fernwirkung der Landschaft als Ganzes und ihrer Formelemente sowie die Polarität zwischen dem Geländeinneren und dem Horizont eine zentrale Rolle.

Jede Architektur ist eine visuelle Beschreibung unseres Verhältnisses zu unserer Umwelt, sie steht im Kontrast natürlicher Bedingungen und kulturtechnischer Reaktionen. Dabei entsteht eine Vielzahl baulicher Artefakte, die von einer komplexen und herausfordernden Beziehung zwischen Mensch und Natur erzählen. Insbesondere die Architektur als zutiefst anthropogene Disziplin ist gefordert, ihre Verantwortung wahrzunehmen und sich mehr für die Themen der Umwelt zu engagieren. Das Darstellen der Landschaft hilft uns, zu verstehen, dass wir nicht auf einem Grundstück bauen, sondern in einem Körper agieren, der aus Schichten, Organismen und Kreisläufen besteht. Architektur ist für uns mehr als ein Objekt vor einem Hintergrund, im besten Fall ist sie wie die Landschaft selbst ein komplexes dynamisches System und eine wandlungsfähige Sphäre, die offen bleibt für Transformation und Entwicklung.

01 Visualisation of unique characteristics in Alpine morphology and composition

Darstellung charakteristischer Merkmale der alpinen Morphologie und Zusammensetzung

02 Visualisation of fall and contour lines

Darstellung von Fall- und Höhenlinien

03 Visualisation of terrain ruggedness

Darstellung der felsigen Geländeoberflächen

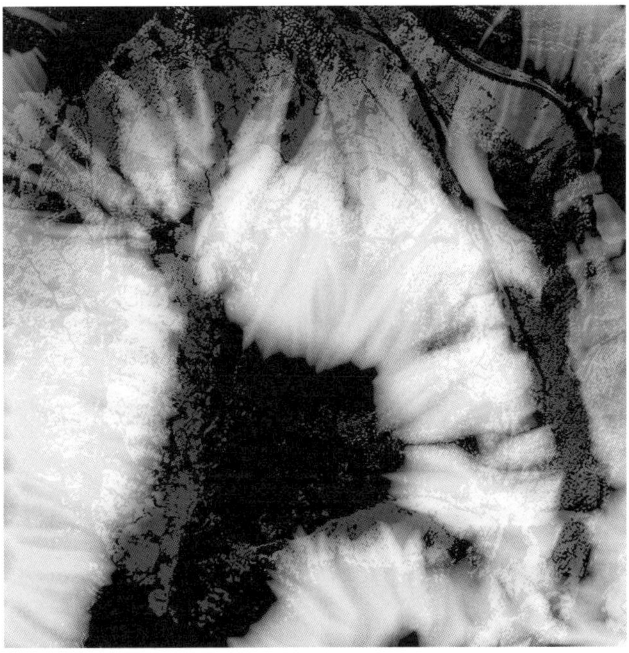

04

Identification of terrain formations by using height maps

Ermittlung von Gelände-formation mittels *height maps*

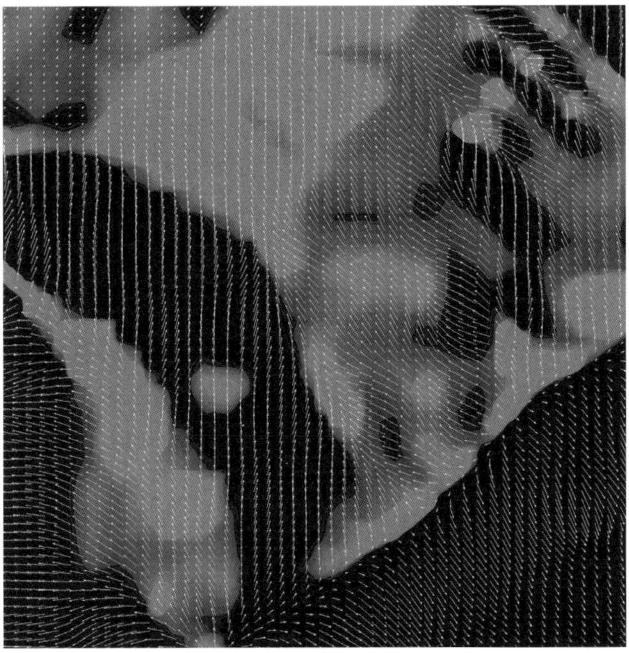

05

Visualisation of slope angles

Visualisierung von Neigungswinkeln

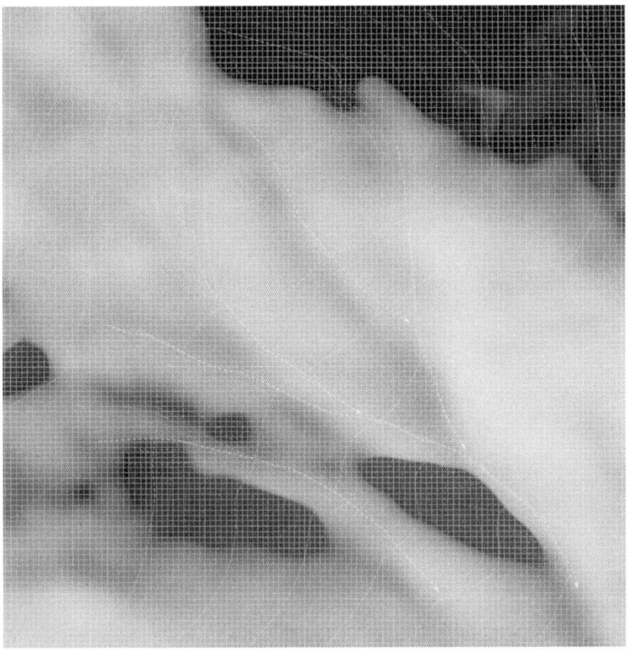

06

Identification of water flows

Ermittlung von Wasserläufen

07

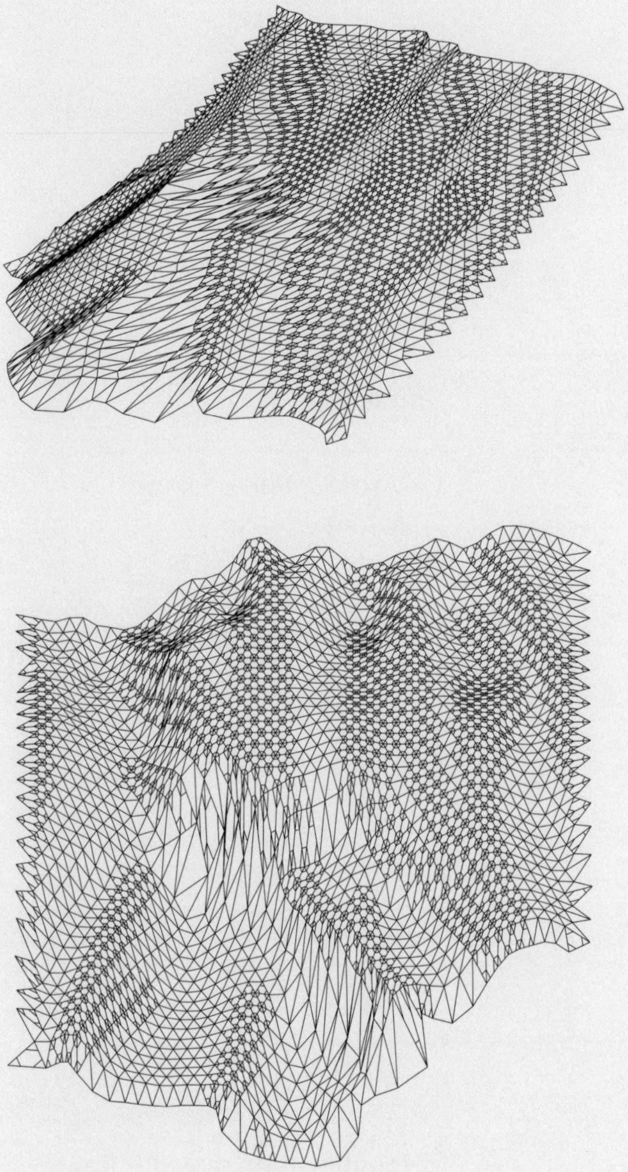

08

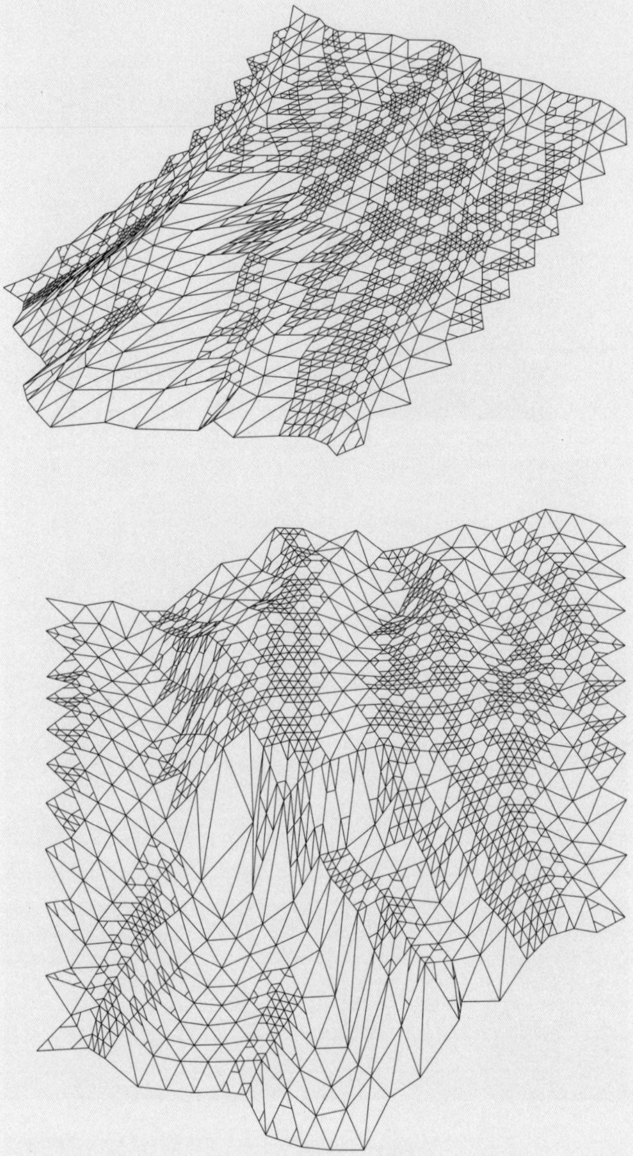

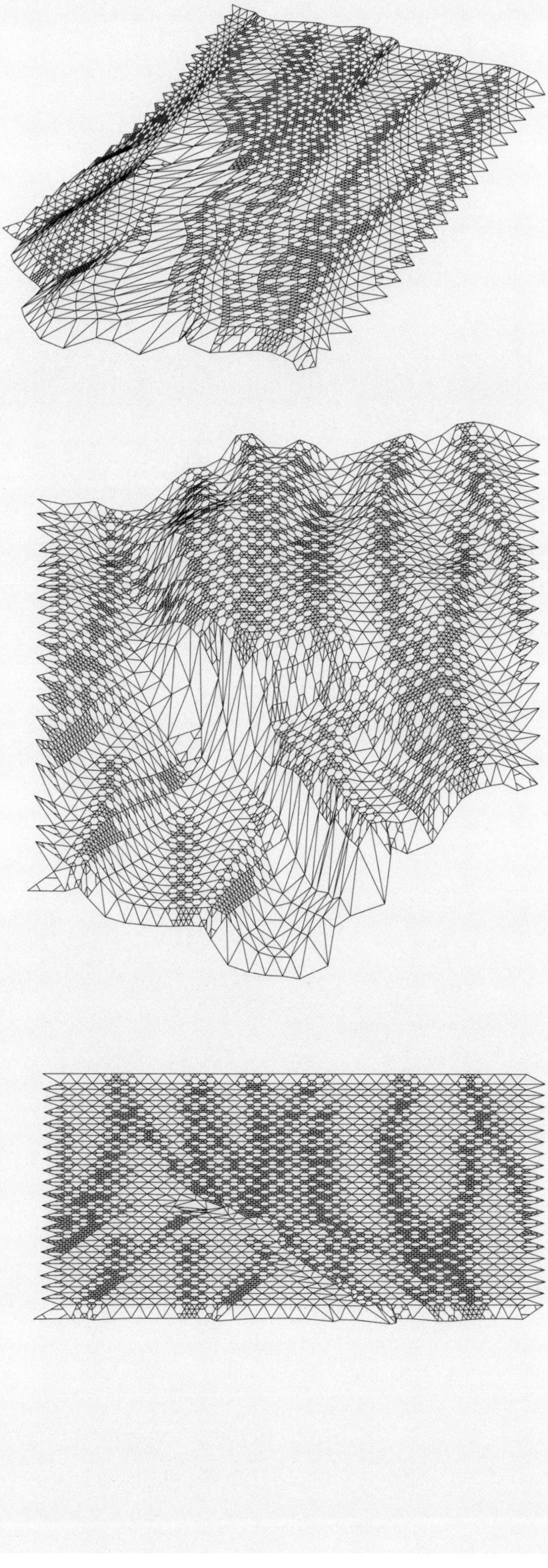

Studies on the tessellation of surfaces

Studien zur Tessellierung von Oberflächen

10 Conversion of grids

Umbau von Netzen

TOP

Top of Tyrol

2008

Viewing platform

Stubai Glacier Austria

"Enveloped in all the nets of its own making, the species constantly watches itself and its artefacts, from an ever-increasing number of angles at every scale, as if fascinated by what it has become."

„Umhüllt von allen Netzen, die sie selbst geschaffen hat, beobachtet die Spezies sich selbst und ihre Artefakte unaufhörlich aus immer mehr Blickwinkeln in jedem Maßstab, als wäre sie fasziniert von dem, was sie geworden ist."

Beatriz Columina & Marc Wigley, *Are We Human? Notes on an Archeology of Design.*

The viewing platform on Großer Isidor is a sketch in the snow, a built form as balancing act. Its architectural concept is based on a geomorphological convergence that seeks a formal balance between the structure itself and the tectonics of the landscape. The contours of this landscape inspire the form, which follows the flowing relief, mediating between the dynamic and the static. Every winter, the ribs disappear for six months below the snow, with only the blades that cantilever out over the Nordwand remaining visible all year round. The wind and the sun expose these steel ribs like lines drawn delicately upon the surface. Transformed by the extreme weather conditions on the glacier, the steel structure offers a foothold to shapes formed from ice and snow.

Die Aussichtsplattform am Großen Isidor ist eine Zeichnung im Schnee, eine Architektur als Gratwandlerin. Ihr architektonisches Konzept beruht auf einer geomorphologischen Annäherung, die ein formales Gleichgewicht zwischen dem Bauwerk und der Tektonik der Landschaft sucht. Das Relief der Landschaft ist formgebend für die Konstruktion, die der fließenden Systematik folgt und zwischen Dynamik und Statik vermittelt. Sechs Monate im Jahr verschwinden die Lamellen im Schnee, nur die über der Nordwand auskragenden Schwerter bleiben das ganze Jahr über sichtbar. Fast wie eine Skizze legen Wind und Sonne die Stahllamellen als zarte Linien an der Oberfläche frei. Die Struktur der Stahlkonstruktion verwandelt sich durch die extreme Witterung des Gletschers und bietet Halt für Formen aus Eis und Schnee.

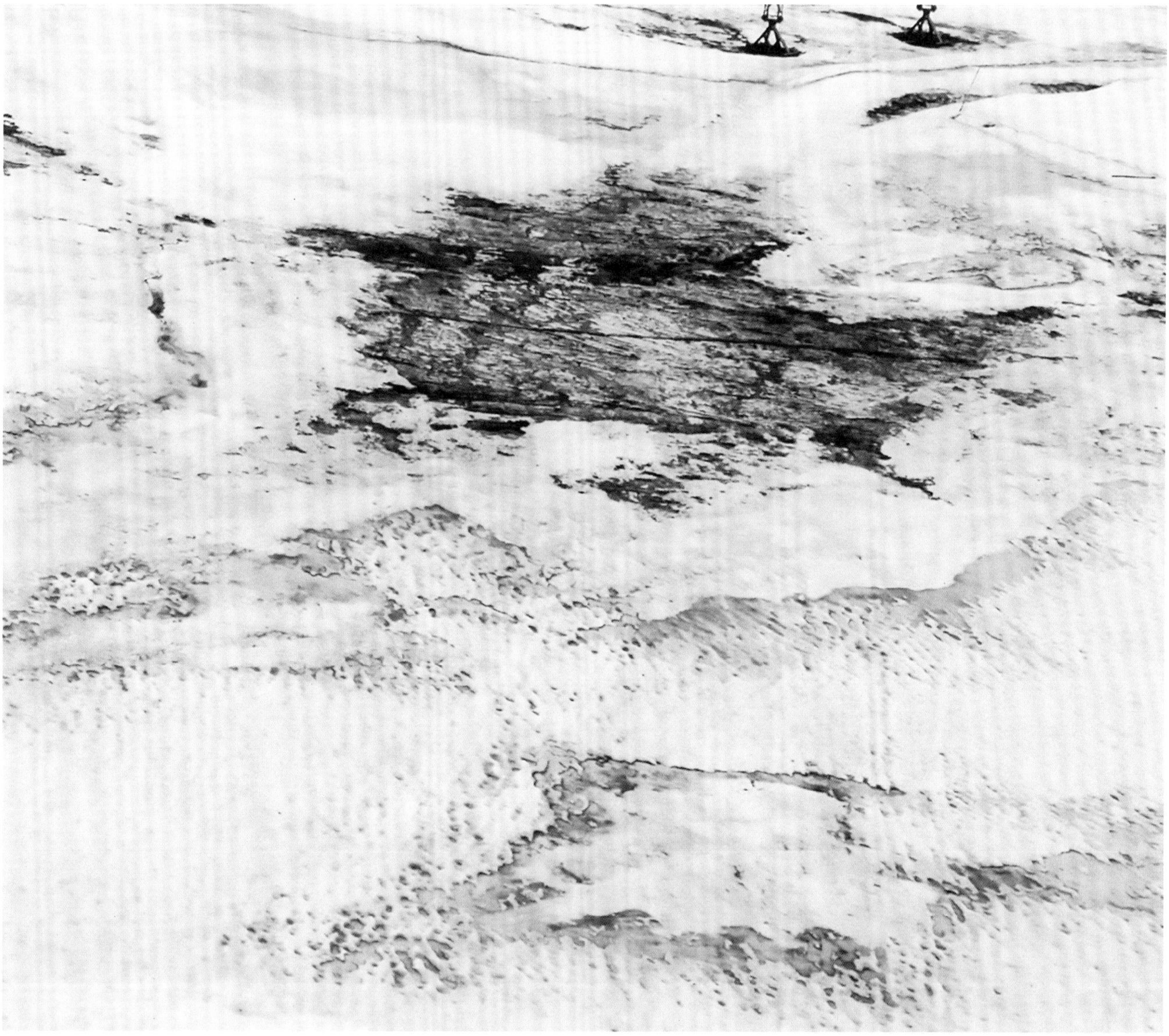

From a geological point of view, we are standing on the ridge of the Schaufeljoch on a fracture pile that primarily consists of metamorphic rocks such as paragneiss and mica schist. On the other hand, we are here in the altitude range of the permafrost lower limit of the Alps, whereby the “cementation” of the rock fragments suffers from higher temperatures and the accompanying thawing of the permafrost.

Aus geologischer Sicht stehen wir am Grat des Schaufeljochs auf einem Bruchhaufen, der überwiegend aus metamorphen Gesteinen wie Paragneis und Glimmerschiefer besteht. Andererseits befinden wir uns hier im Höhenbereich der Permafrost-Untergrenze der Alpen, wobei die „Zementierung“ der Gesteinsbrocken unter höheren Temperaturen und dem damit einhergehenden Auftauen des Permafrosts leidet.

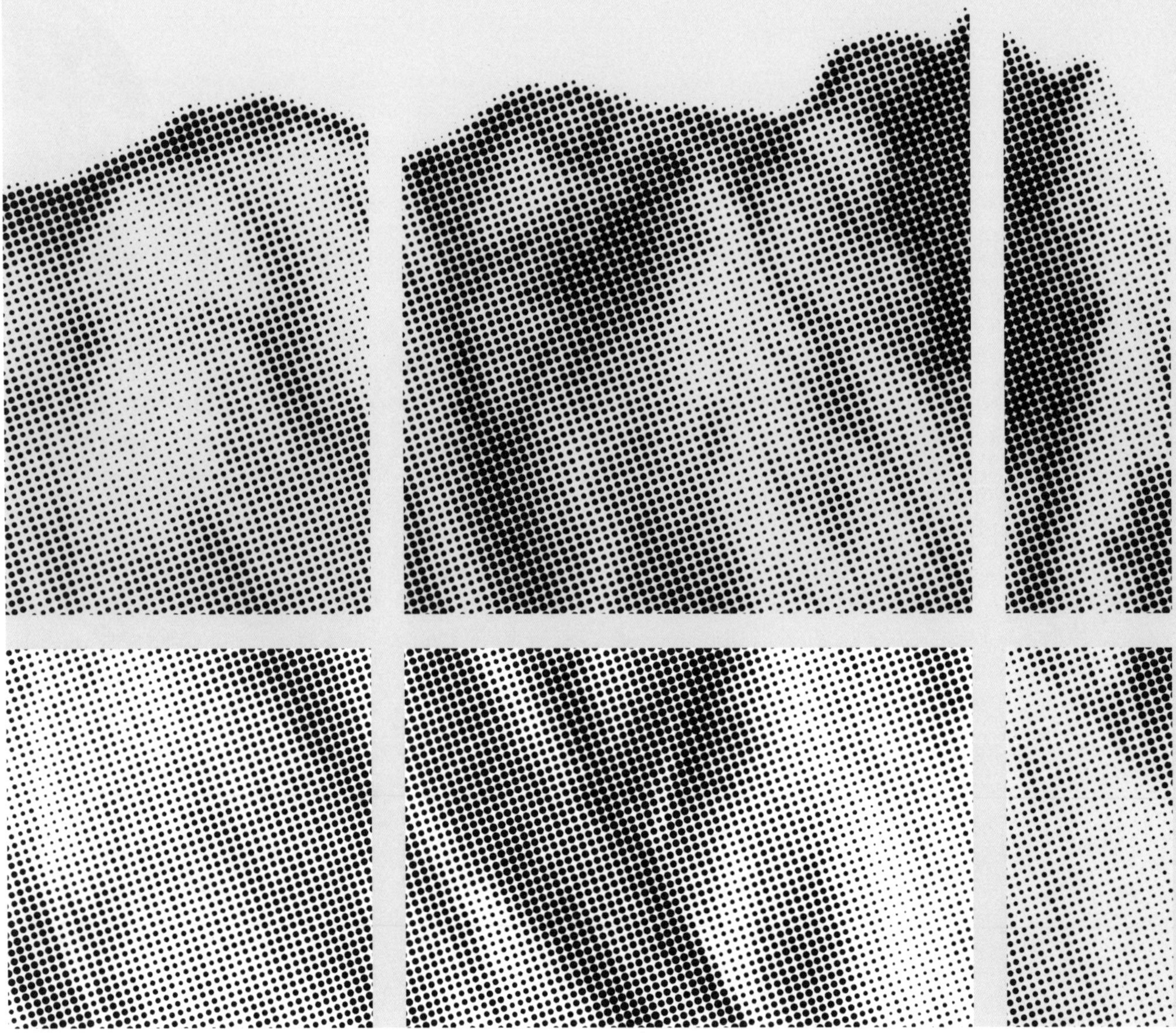

Platform structure

Struktur der Plattform

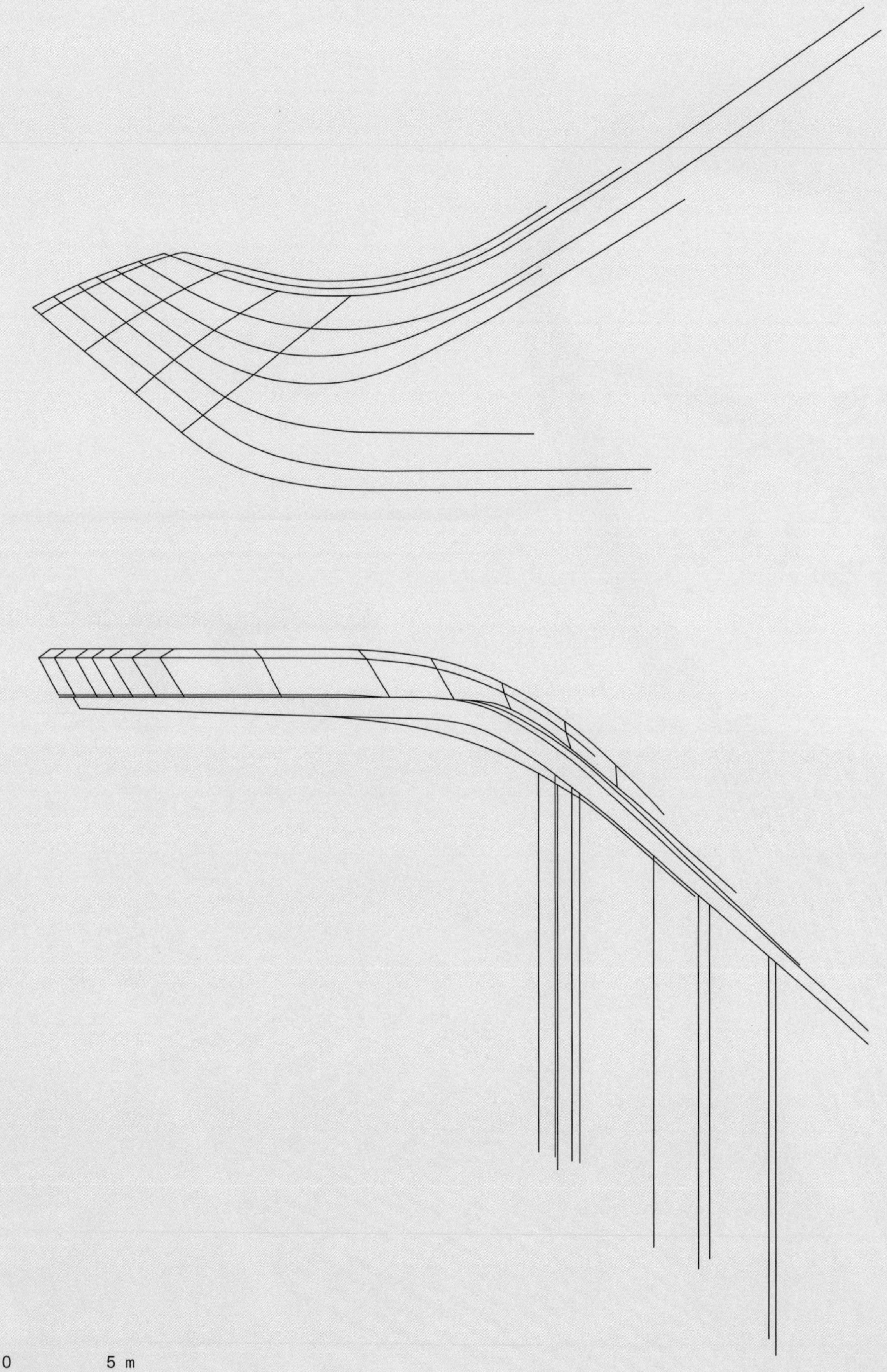

How long does the figure-ground relationship between mass and diagram last?

Wie lange hält die Figur-Grund-Beziehung zwischen Masse und Diagramm noch?

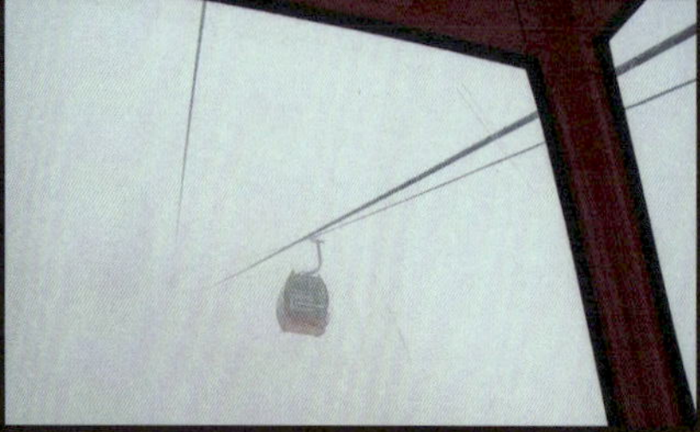

NORTHLAND

WINNEBACH

NPO	Nature on Stage	2015	Exhibition architecture	Nature Park Ötztal Austria
PROJECT	TITLE	YEAR	SUBJECT	LOCATION

"Most natural disasters are characteristic rather than accidental features of the places and societies where they occur"; these words from the geographer Kenneth Hewitt perfectly describe the landscape situation in the Ötztal Valley.

The cultural development of the valley is shaped by its extreme topography, the climatic conditions and a landscape that is changing in every respect. It is rooted in a historical narrative that tells of challenges and adaptation. The structures in the Ötztal Nature Park are furniture-like fragments of landscape, which pick up on this contrast between natural conditions and cultural and technical reactions and reconcile the protection of nature from humans with the protection of humans from nature.

„Most natural disasters are characteristic rather than accidental features of the places and societies where they occur", mit diesem Satz des Geografen Kenneth Hewitt lässt sich die landschaftsräumliche Situation des Ötztals trefflich beschreiben.

Die kulturelle Entwicklung des Ötztals wird geprägt von einer extremen Topografie, den klimatischen Bedingungen und einer sich allseits im Wandel befindlichen Landschaft. Sie basiert auf einer Entstehungsgeschichte, die von Herausforderungen und Anpassung erzählt. Die Naturparkstrukturen im Ötztal sind möbelhafte Landschaftsfragmente, die diesen Kontrast zwischen natürlichen Bedingungen und kulturtechnischen Reaktionen aufgreifen und den Schutz der Natur vor dem Menschen mit dem Schutz des Menschen vor der Natur verhandeln.

BESONDERE ORTE /
SPECIAL PLACES
NATURPARK ÖTZTAL
RELIEF /
RELIEF

The primary construction of this exhibition object translates the topography of the landscape around Niederthai as a mesh. The mesh picks up on the specific event of the rock fall and highlights it as a sculptural element.

Die Primärkonstruktion dieses Ausstellungsobjekts übersetzt die Topografie der Landschaft rund um Niederthai als Netz. Das Netz greift das konkrete Ereignis des Bergsturzes auf und hebt es als skulpturales Element hervor.

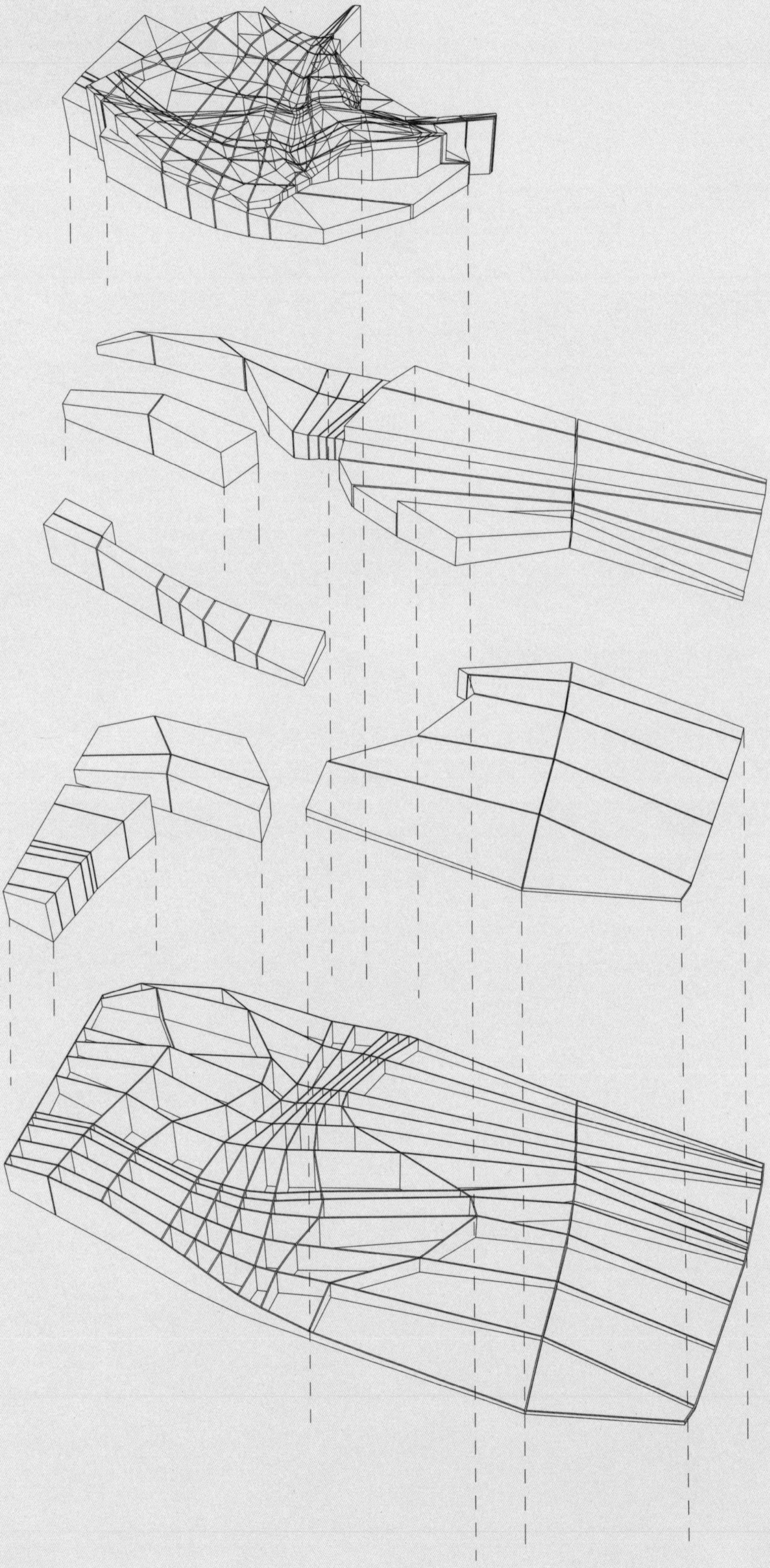

Display Gries

The primary construction of this exhibition object translates the topography of the landscape around Gries as a mesh. The mesh focuses on the torrent as a characteristic element and forms it into a sculptural object.

Die Primärkonstruktion dieses Ausstellungsobjekts übersetzt die Topografie der Grieser Landschaft in ein Netz. Das Netz fokussiert den Wildbach als charakteristisches Element und formt ihn zu einem skulpturalen Objekt.

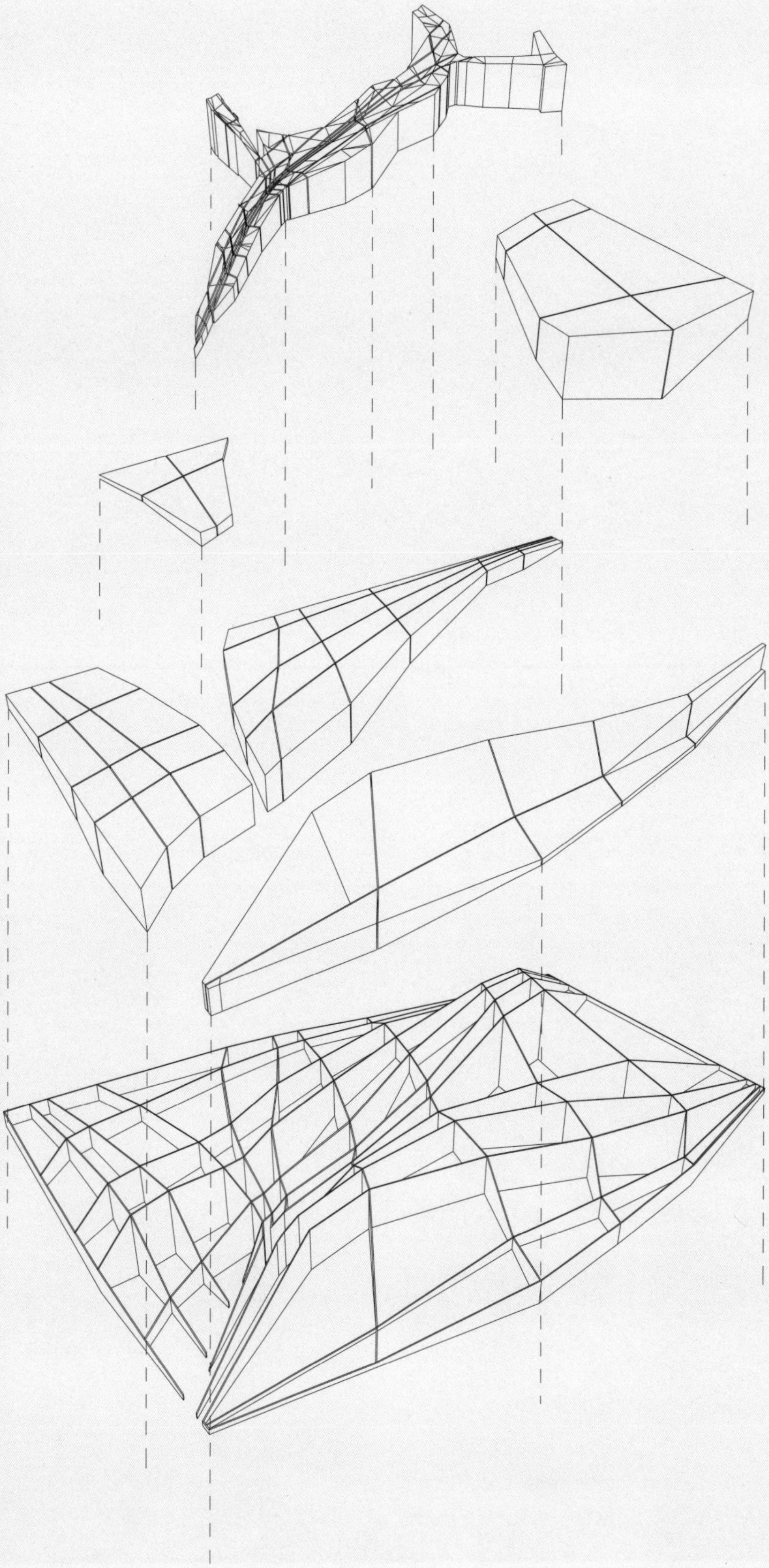

TAUFERBERG
AUSSICHTSPLATTFORMEN / VIEWING PLATFORMS

Topographic mesh model Umhausen district

Topografisches Netzmodell Bezirk Umhausen

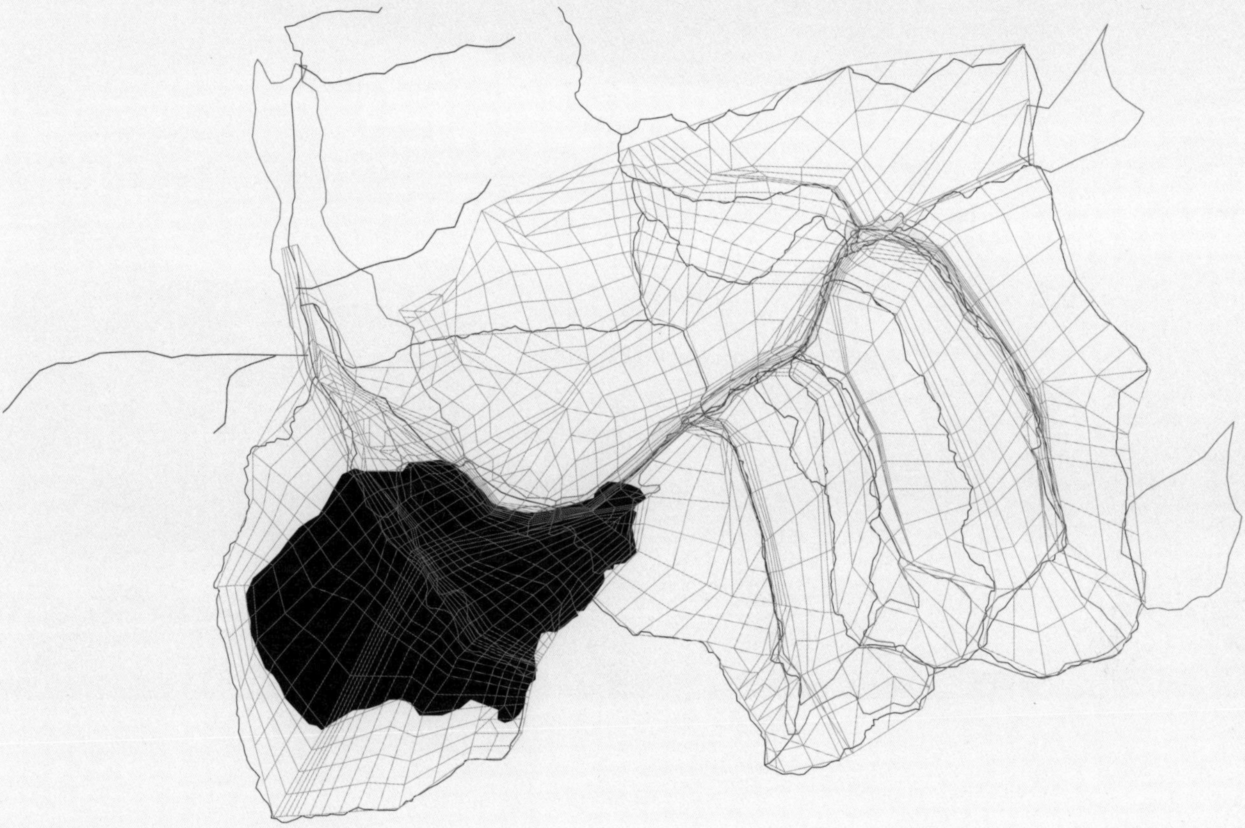

The Tauferberg is a rock mass that was formed by the Köfler rockfall about 8000 years ago. During this natural event, about 2-3 km^3 of rock mass moved down to the valley and spread over an area of about 12 km^2. According to British scientists Alan Bond and Mark Hempsell, the rockfall was caused by a comet impact.

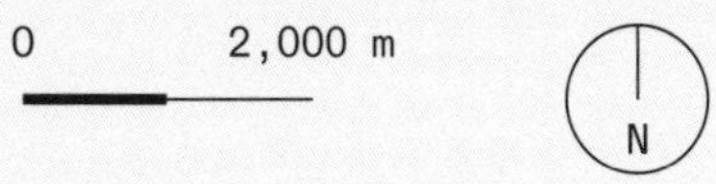

Der Tauferberg ist eine Felsmasse, die durch den Köfler Bergsturz vor etwa 8000 Jahren entstanden ist. Bei diesem Naturereignis bewegten sich ca. 2-3 km^3 Bergsturzmasse in Richtung Tal und verteilten sich auf eine Fläche von ca. 12 km^2. Laut den britischen Wissenschaftlern Alan Bond und Mark Hempsell wurde der Felsabbruch durch einen Kometeneinschlag verursacht.

FISCHBACH

SYNTHETIC LANDSCAPES

AN ARCHITECTURAL CONTRIBUTION TO CLIMATE CHANGE

Claudia Pasquero

Contemporary design is plural, collective and mutant. In times of global climate change we are told no ecosystem is unaffected by human actions. But which kind of change are we referring to? Are not change, transformation and adaptation all inherent qualities of the planet we inhabit?

Our current stage of technological evolution is opening scenarios where traditional dichotomies such as natural and artificial, material and digital, human and non-human become obsolete.

If, for example, we look at large growing cities from a satellite, we realise that it is becoming increasingly difficult to define what is natural and what is artificial. From this perspective, global cities – despite being large artificial systems often depicted as the antithesis of nature – develop patterns of growth or shrinkage that recall natural formations of a radically different kind.

Cities appear as complex synthetic organisms. This perspective contradicts the model of urbanity that we inherited from modernity, where zones are clearly defined and morphologically demarcated.

LAAC transfers this synthetic understanding of the environment to the Alpine landscape by investigating the integration of renewable energy sources into the landscape in what the architectural practice has titled *Sustainable Design for Alpine Infrastructures* and engaged with as a research-based project. As a spatial planning tool, they propose a zoning plan that uses climate, weather and terrain data to map a distribution pattern that blurs the boundaries between natural systems and artificial ones, between inhabitable landscape and infrastructure.

The current energy crisis underlines the need for growing and harvesting to open up possibilities for more ecological design strategies in contrast to the ongoing mining of the earth's crust and its resources.

The Alps recall idyllic portraits of unspoiled nature, featuring peaks, glaciers, lakes and pastures. Yet, perhaps paradoxically, the Alps are also a surprisingly poignant reflection of the effects of climate change and the current conceptual, political and practical inability of our society to deal with them. Retreating glaciers are the most striking phenomenon of all; they are formations of geological time that are melting in front of our eyes in a matter of years.

Standing on LAAC's viewing platform on the Stubai Glacier, we not only look at an impressive 360-degree mountain panorama, but also witness the drastic transformation of the glacier and its dying body, which we desperately conceal with white blankets, more to ease the pain for its loss than to protect it.

The platform itself is the result of precisely determined data that provide information about the geomorphological composition of the mountain formation on the one hand and the permafrost that is disappearing on the other. Like a prosthesis, the platform holds the mountain together to enable us to physically become part of a geological transformation, and therefore allow us to understand it and eventually interact with it in a deeper and more complex manner.

Beyond melancholy we can find refuge in the cold belly of pure science, systematically drilling cores in the deep ice before it is gone. In the strata, literally frozen in time, is a repository of the Alpine microclimate, including human inhabitation's effects on it. An enormous amount of data is stored in particles and molecules of air trapped in the layers of ice, every layer a year of history, a cycle of life.

Decoding these data reveals a bio-computational Alpine panorama, composed of exponentially increasing carbon dioxide concentrations, unique diversity of contaminants and intense metabolic activity. These abstract depictions can be actualised through architectural interventions at multiple scales, by testing ways to influence those processes that are currently causing the rapid retreat of glaciers. Architecture as a discipline seeks to intervene at the molecular scale of particles and crystals, the mesoscale of pastoral communities and the macroscale of renewable energy networks.

Through drawings, models, prototypes, videos and installations, LAAC's landscape architectural projects question and make tangible, at the same time, the material, morphological and social nature of climate change in the Alpine space.

Such questioning has global relevance, well beyond the specific aspects and solutions of individual case studies; and that is because media scaremongering as well as the hard scientific evidence measured in centigrade and tonnes of CO_2 have failed in their ambition to create global consensus and trigger actions. On the contrary, they have contributed to a climate of increased ideological confrontation. Another tactic is necessary, other tools are required, and I am convinced that architects and urban designers have something to contribute here, with multidimensional, transdisciplinary and ideologically unbiased depictions of the nature of climate change.

Das zeitgenössische Design ist vielseitig, gemeinschaftlich und verändert sich ständig. In Zeiten des weltweiten Klimawandels wird uns vermittelt, dass kein Ökosystem von menschlichem Handeln unberührt ist. Aber um welche Art des Wandels handelt es sich? Sind denn nicht Wandel, Transformation und Anpassung naturgegebene Qualitäten des Planeten, den wir bewohnen?

Unser aktueller Zustand technologischer Evolution eröffnet Szenarien, bei denen traditionelle Gegensätze wie natürlich und künstlich, materiell und digital, menschlich und nicht menschlich überholt erscheinen.

Wenn wir beispielsweise große wachsende Städte aus der Satellitenperspektive betrachten, stellen wir fest, dass es zunehmend schwieriger wird, zu bestimmen, was natürlich und was künstlich ist. Obwohl sie riesige künstliche Systeme sind, die oft als Antithese zur Natur dargestellt werden, so entwickeln globale Städte aus dieser Perspektive Wachstums- oder auch Schrumpfmuster, die an natürliche Formationen einer gänzlich anderen Art erinnern.

Städte erscheinen als komplexe synthetische Organismen. Diese Perspektive widerspricht dem Städtemodell, das wir von der Moderne übernommen haben, bei dem die einzelnen Bereiche klar definiert und morphologisch abgegrenzt sind.

LAAC übertragen dieses synthetische Verständnis von Umwelt auf die alpine Landschaft, indem sie die Einbindung von erneuerbaren Energiequellen in die Landschaft untersuchen, unter dem Titel *Nachhaltiges Design alpiner*

Strukturen, verbunden mit einem forschungsbasierten Projekt. Als Raumplanungsinstrument schlagen sie einen Flächenwidmungsplan vor, der Klima, Wetter und Geländedaten verwendet, um ein Verteilungsmuster zu entwerfen, das die Grenzen zwischen natürlichen und künstlichen Systemen, zwischen bewohnbaren Landschaften und Infrastruktur verschwimmen lässt.

Die aktuelle Energiekrise unterstreicht die Notwendigkeit von Wachstum und Ernte und eröffnet Möglichkeiten für vermehrt ökologische Entwurfsstrategien im Vergleich zum anhaltenden Abbau der Erdkruste und ihrer Ressourcen.

Die Alpen erinnern an idyllische Bilder unberührter Natur, mit Bergspitzen, Gletschern, Seen und Weidegebieten. Und dennoch sind die Alpen, wahrscheinlich auf paradoxe Art, auch eine überraschend schmerzliche Reflexion der Auswirkungen des Klimawandels und der gegenwärtigen gedanklichen, politischen und praktischen Unfähigkeit unserer Gesellschaft, mit ihnen umzugehen. Schwindende Gletscher sind dabei das auffälligste Phänomen; als Formationen eines geologischen Zeitalters schmelzen sie in nur wenigen Jahren vor unseren Augen dahin.

Wenn wir auf der LAAC-Aussichtsplattform auf dem Stubaier Gletscher stehen, sehen wir nicht nur ein beeindruckendes 360-Grad-Bergpanorama, sondern wir sind auch Zeug*innen der drastischen Veränderung des Gletschers und seines Sterbens, das wir verzweifelt mit weißen Tüchern verbergen, wohl eher um den Verlustschmerz zu lindern, als den Gletscher zu schützen.

Die Plattform selbst ist das Ergebnis von genau ermittelten Daten, die einerseits Auskunft über die geomorphologische Zusammensetzung der Gebirgsbildung und andererseits über den schwindenden Permafrost geben. Wie eine Prothese hält die Plattform den Berg zusammen und ermöglicht uns, auf nahezu körperliche Art ein Teil der geologischen Veränderung zu werden. So können wir diese verstehen und letztlich auf eine tiefere und komplexere Art auf sie einwirken.

Jenseits von Melancholie können wir Zuflucht im kalten Magen der reinen Wissenschaft finden, indem wir systematisch Löcher in das tiefe Eis bohren, bevor es verschwunden ist. In den Schichten, die buchstäblich in der Zeit eingefroren sind, befindet sich ein Speicher des alpinen Mikroklimas. Dabei sind die Auswirkungen der menschlichen Einflussnahme miteingeschlossen – eine unglaubliche Datenmenge, gespeichert in den Teilchen und Luftmolekülen, die in den Eisschichten eingefangen sind. Jede Schicht entspricht einem Geschichtsjahr, einem Lebenszyklus.

Die Entschlüsselung dieser Daten bringt ein biorechnerisches alpines Panorama zutage, das sich aus exponentiell ansteigenden Kohlendioxidkonzentrationen, einer einzigartigen Palette von Schmutzstoffen und intensiver metabolischer Aktivität zusammensetzt. Diese abstrakten Darstellungen können durch architektonische Interventionen auf verschiedenen Ebenen konkretisiert werden, indem Möglichkeiten erprobt werden, wie jene Prozesse, die derzeit den raschen Rückgang der Gletscher verursachen, beeinflusst werden können. Die Architektur als Disziplin versucht zu intervenieren, und zwar auf der molekularen Ebene der Partikel und Kristalle, der Mesoebene der ländlichen Gemeinschaften und der Makroebene von Netzwerken für erneuerbare Energie.

Durch Zeichnungen, Modelle, Prototypen, Videos und Installationen hinterfragen die architektonischen Landschaftsprojekte von LAAC die materielle, morphologische und soziale Natur des Klimawandels im alpinen Raum und machen sie dadurch gleichzeitig für uns erfahrbar.

Diese Fragestellungen haben eine globale Relevanz, die weit über die besonderen Aspekte und Lösungen von einzelnen Fallstudien hinausgeht – und dies deshalb, weil sowohl die Panikmache der Medien als auch die wissenschaftlichen Beweise, die in Celsius und CO_2-Mengen gemessen werden, in ihrer Absicht gescheitert sind, einen globalen Konsens herzustellen, um Gegenmaßnahmen auszulösen. Im Gegenteil – sie haben zu einem Klima der ideologischen Konfrontation beigetragen. Eine andere Taktik wäre daher notwendig, andere Hilfsmittel werden benötigt, und ich bin überzeugt, dass Architekt*innen und Städteplaner*innen hier einen wichtigen Beitrag leisten können, nämlich mit multidimensionalen, transdisziplinären und ideologisch neutralen Darstellungen der Erscheinungsform des Klimawandels.

Claudia Pasquero is an architect, curator, author and educator; her work and research operate at the intersection of biology, computation and design. She is co-founder of ecoLogicStudio in London, Landscape Architecture Professor at Innsbruck University and Associated Professor at the Bartlett UCL.

Claudia has been Head Curator of the Tallinn Architectural Biennale 2017 and she has been nominated in the WIRED smart list in the same year.

She is co-author of *Systemic Architecture – Operating Manual for the Self-Organizing City* and she is currently co-authoring her latest book, *DeepGreen, Bio-Design in the Age of Artificial Intelligence,* due to be published in summer 2023.

Her work has been exhibited internationally: at the Centre Pompidou in Paris, the Design Museum in London, the Venice Architectural Biennale, the Mori Museum in Tokyo, ZKM Karlsruhe, the Saudi Art Biennale in Riyadh and COP26 in Glasgow, among others. ecoLogicStudio has successfully completed a series of photosynthetic architectures, such as the Urban Algae Folly Milano 2015, the BioTechHut Astana 2017, PhotoSynthEtica Dublin 2019, PhotosSynthEtica Helsinki 2020, AirBubble Playground Warsaw 2021, etc.

Claudia Pasquero ist Architektin, Kuratorin, Autorin und Pädagogin. Ihre Arbeit und ihre Forschung bewegen sich an der Schnittstelle von Biologie, Computersimulation und Design. Sie ist Mitbegründerin von ecoLogicStudio in London, Professorin für Landschaftsarchitektur an der Universität Innsbruck und assoziierte Professorin am Bartlett UCL.

Claudia war Chefkuratorin der Architekturbiennale Tallinn 2017 und wurde im selben Jahr für die WIRED Smart List nominiert.

Sie ist Co-Autorin von *Systemic Architecture – Operating Manual for the Self-Organizing City* und arbeitet derzeit an ihrem neuesten Buch, *DeepGreen, Bio-Design in the Age of Artificial Intelligence*, das im Sommer 2023 erscheinen soll.

Ihre Arbeiten wurden international ausgestellt: im Centre Pompidou in Paris, im Design Museum in London, auf der Architekturbiennale in Venedig, im Mori Museum in Tokio, im ZKM Karlsruhe, auf der Saudi Art Biennale in Riad, auf der COP26 in Glasgow etc. ecoLogicStudio hat erfolgreich eine Reihe von fotosynthetischen Architekturen realisiert, z.B. die Urban Algae Folly Milano 2015, die BioTechHut Astana 2017, PhotoSynthEtica Dublin 2019, PhotosSynthEtica Helsinki 2020, AirBubble Playground Warsaw 2021.

SDI	Sustainable Design for Alpine Infra-structures	2015	Alpine power plants	Alpine space Austria
PROJECT	TITLE	YEAR	SUBJECT	LOCATION

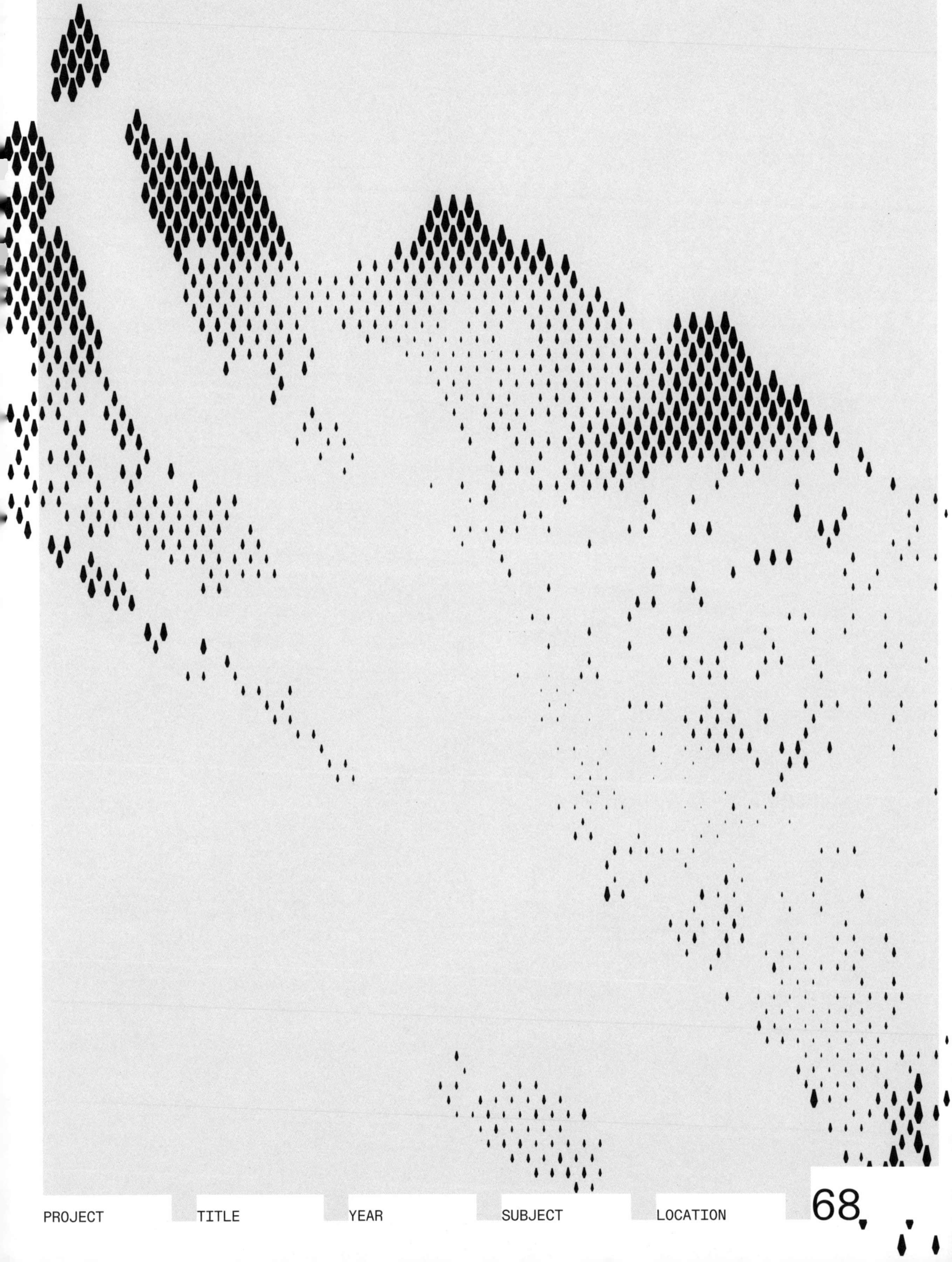

The research project *Sustainable Design for Alpine Infrastructures* addresses the challenges of the energy transition. The realignment from fossil fuels and atomic power towards renewable energies is already happening, all around the globe. The advantages of renewables are already well known and the rapid expansion of their use is supported by a broad swathe of the population. But while such facilities are easy to build in lower-lying regions, the sensitive and environmentally friendly integration of renewable energy sources into natural Alpine locations represents a huge challenge in terms of environmental design. And one of the few yet very powerful disadvantages of such projects is the need to intervene in a natural setting. An analysis of the latest research suggests that the sustainability debate is principally focused on climate- and resource-friendly solutions and energy efficiency. The question of integration into the landscape remains largely unaddressed. This one-sided approach will guarantee neither the public acceptance of such interventions, nor the quality of the resulting recreational and living environment.

The project includes extensive studies of potential and compatible locations and of distribution patterns for the elements of such power stations. It also investigates and pushes ahead with the technological development of energy sources that are particularly suitable for Alpine locations. One example of the output from the project is the zoning plans, which, by defining the location and the basic form of sites for wind and solar power plants, can play a role as instruments of land-use planning.

Das Forschungsprojekt *Sustainable Design for Alpine Infrastructures* befasst sich mit Herausforderungen der Energiewende. Eine Umorientierung weg von fossilen Energieträgern und Kernkraft hin zu erneuerbaren Energien findet bereits weltweit statt. Die Vorteile erneuerbarer Energien sind bestens bekannt und der rasche Ausbau wird von einer breiten Bevölkerung mitgetragen. Während der Bau dieser Anlagen im außeralpinen Raum leicht zu bewältigen ist, stellt die sensible und umweltverträgliche Integration erneuerbarer Energieträger in den alpinen Naturraum im Sinne eines Umweltdesigns eine große Herausforderung dar. Einer der wenigen, aber markanten Nachteile sind die damit verbundenen notwendigen Eingriffe in die Natur. Betrachtet man den Forschungsstand der Entwicklung, so fällt auf, dass unter Nachhaltigkeit vor allem Klima- und Ressourcenverträglichkeit sowie die Energieeffizienz thematisiert werden. Die Frage der Integration ins Landschaftsbild bleibt weitgehend unbehandelt. Durch diese einseitige Vorgehensweise kann weder eine Akzeptanz seitens der Bevölkerung erreicht noch die Qualität als Erholungs- und Lebensraum gewährleistet werden.

Das Projekt beinhaltet umfangreiche Studien über mögliche und verträgliche Standorte sowie die Form von Verteilungsmustern solcher Kraftwerke. Ebenso wird die technologische Entwicklung geeigneter Energieträger speziell für alpine Lagen untersucht und vorangetrieben. Das Ergebnis könnten beispielsweise Flächenwidmungspläne sein, welche Standorte und Form von Baufeldern für Wind und Solarkraftwerke definieren und dadurch als Raumordnungsinstrumente fungieren.

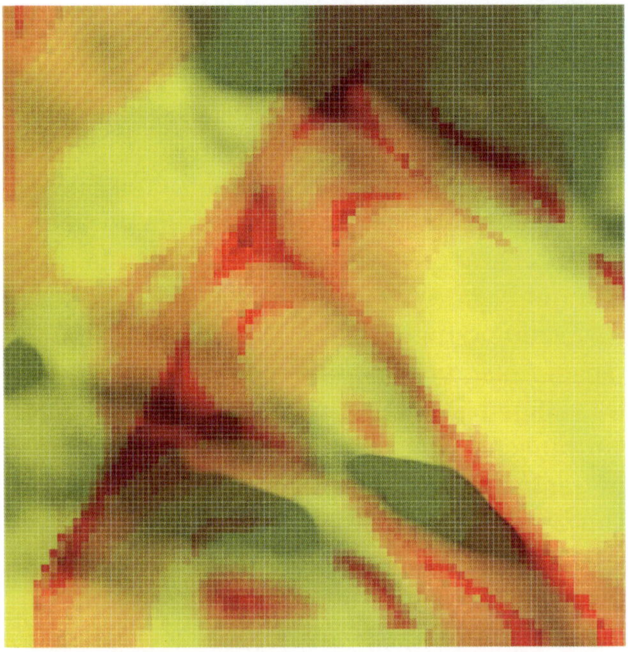

01

Solar exposure on 1 July

Solare Exposition am 1. Juli

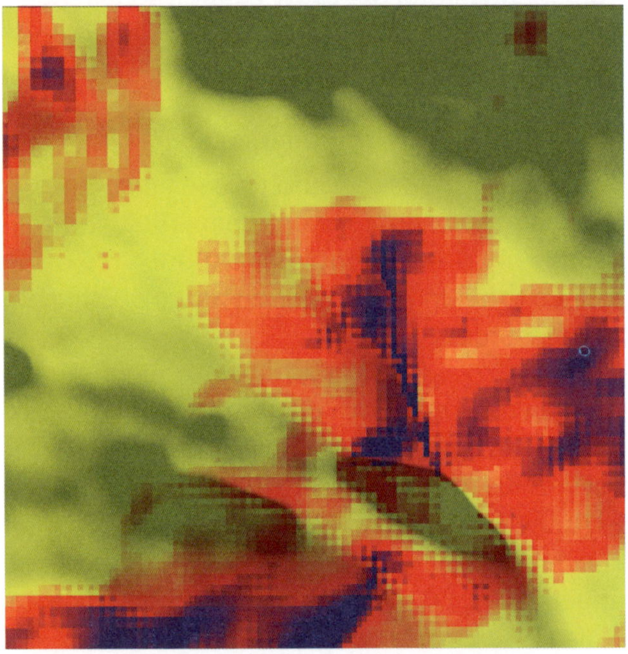

02

Solar exposure on 1 January

Solare Exposition am 1. Januar

03

Average annual solar input

Durchschnittlicher solarer Jahreseintrag

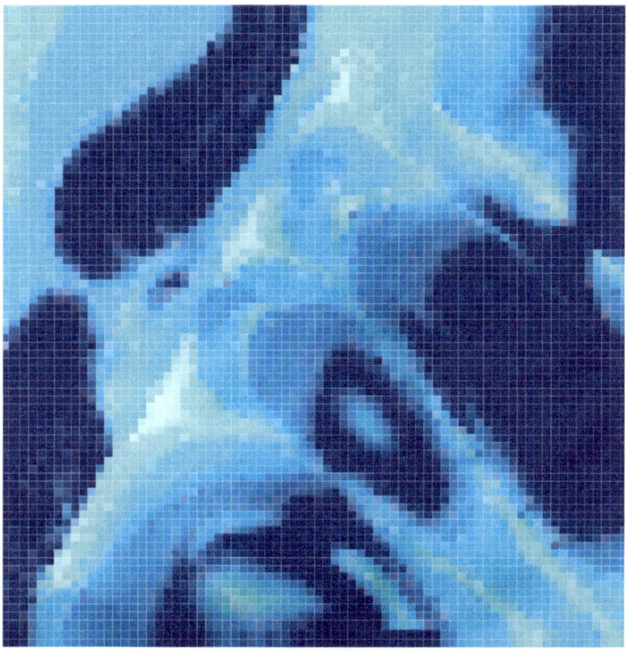

04 Average annual wind exposition

Durchschnittliche jährliche Windexposition

05 Average annual solar input

Durchschnittlicher jährlicher Windeintrag

06 Wind and solar field in winter

Wind- und Solarfeld im Winter

07

Studies on hexagonal solar panels

Systemstudie zu sechseckigen Solarmodulen

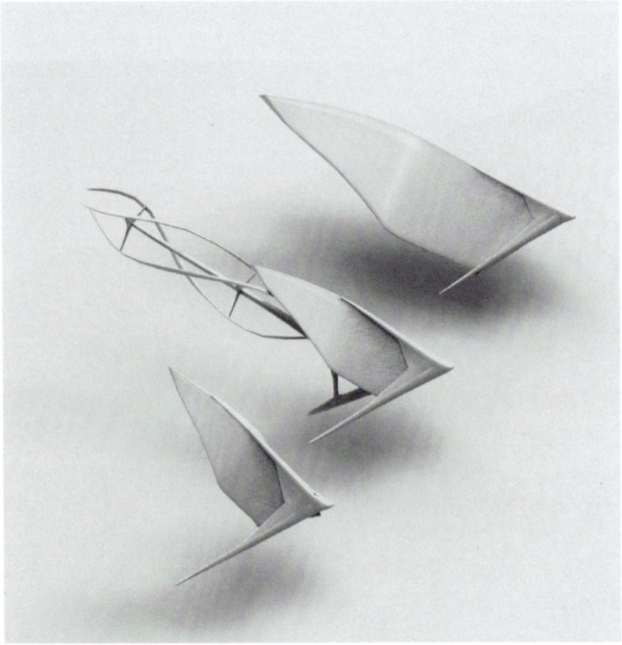

08

Studies on wind energy field elements

Studien zu Windenergiefeld-elementen

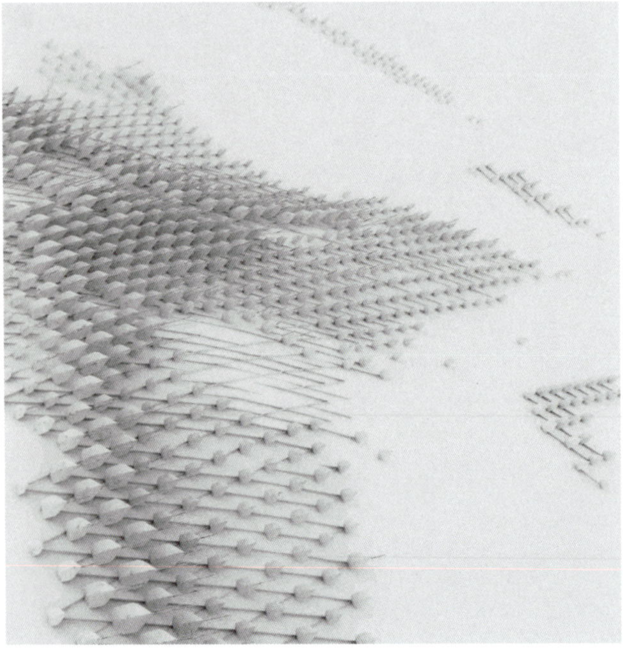

09

Distribution pattern of an energy field

Verteilungsmuster eines Energiefeldes

10

Zoning plan for wind and solar energy fields

Flächenwidmungsplan für Solar- und Windenergiefelder

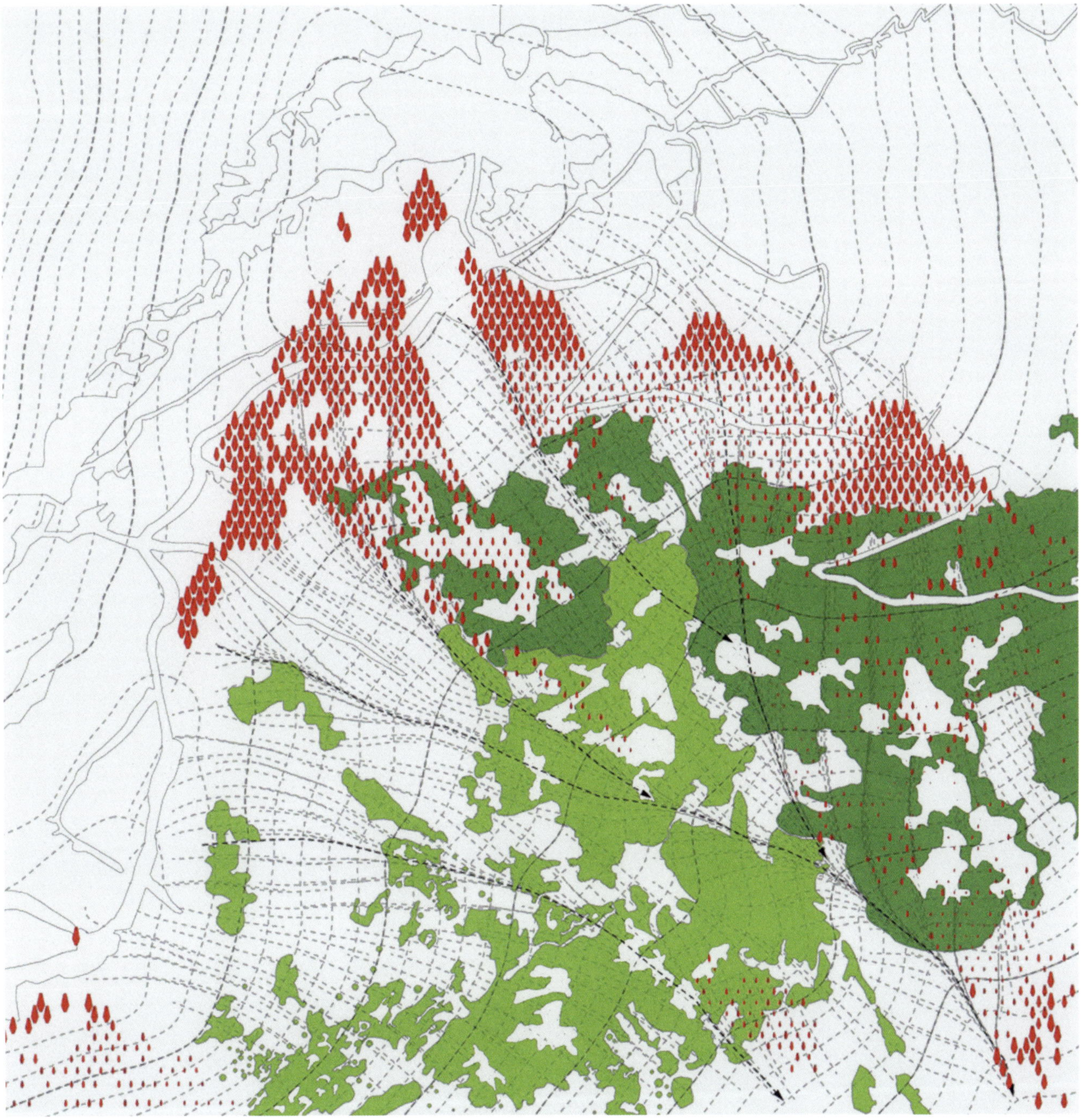

CCN | Copa Cagrana | 2018 | Urban beach | Vienna Austria

PROJECT TITLE YEAR SUBJECT LOCATION

The creation of the over 20-km-long Donauinsel as both a flood protection barrier and a leisure area is one of Vienna's most sustainable achievements. As an interface between local residents and recreational visitors, Copa Cagrana embodies the cultural self-image of a city with an increasingly diverse society.

This is now the setting for a remodelling of the riverbank as a docking station for urban diversity, in which Vienna's broad range of social milieux, ethnic groups and ideologies can come together. In this spirit, the robust green foundation of the newly shaped space takes the extremely open approach of seeking to determine little and facilitate a lot.

Die Entstehung der über 20 Kilometer langen Donauinsel als Hochwasserschutz- und Naherholungsgebiet zählt zu den nachhaltigsten Errungenschaften Wiens. Als Schnittstelle zwischen Anwohner*innen und Erholungssuchenden steht die Copa Cagrana exemplarisch für das kulturelle Selbstverständnis einer Stadt mit einer zunehmend diversen Gesellschaft.

An dieser Schnittstelle artikuliert die neue Ufergestaltung eine Dockingstation urbaner Diversität, an der unterschiedliche soziale Milieus, Ethnien und Ideologien Anschluss finden. Das neu geformte Terrain, ein robustes grünes Fundament, agiert in diesem Sinne freimütig, versucht, wenig zu bestimmen und viel zu ermöglichen.

Distribution of the building masses on the riverside

Verteilung der Gebäudevolumen am Flussufer

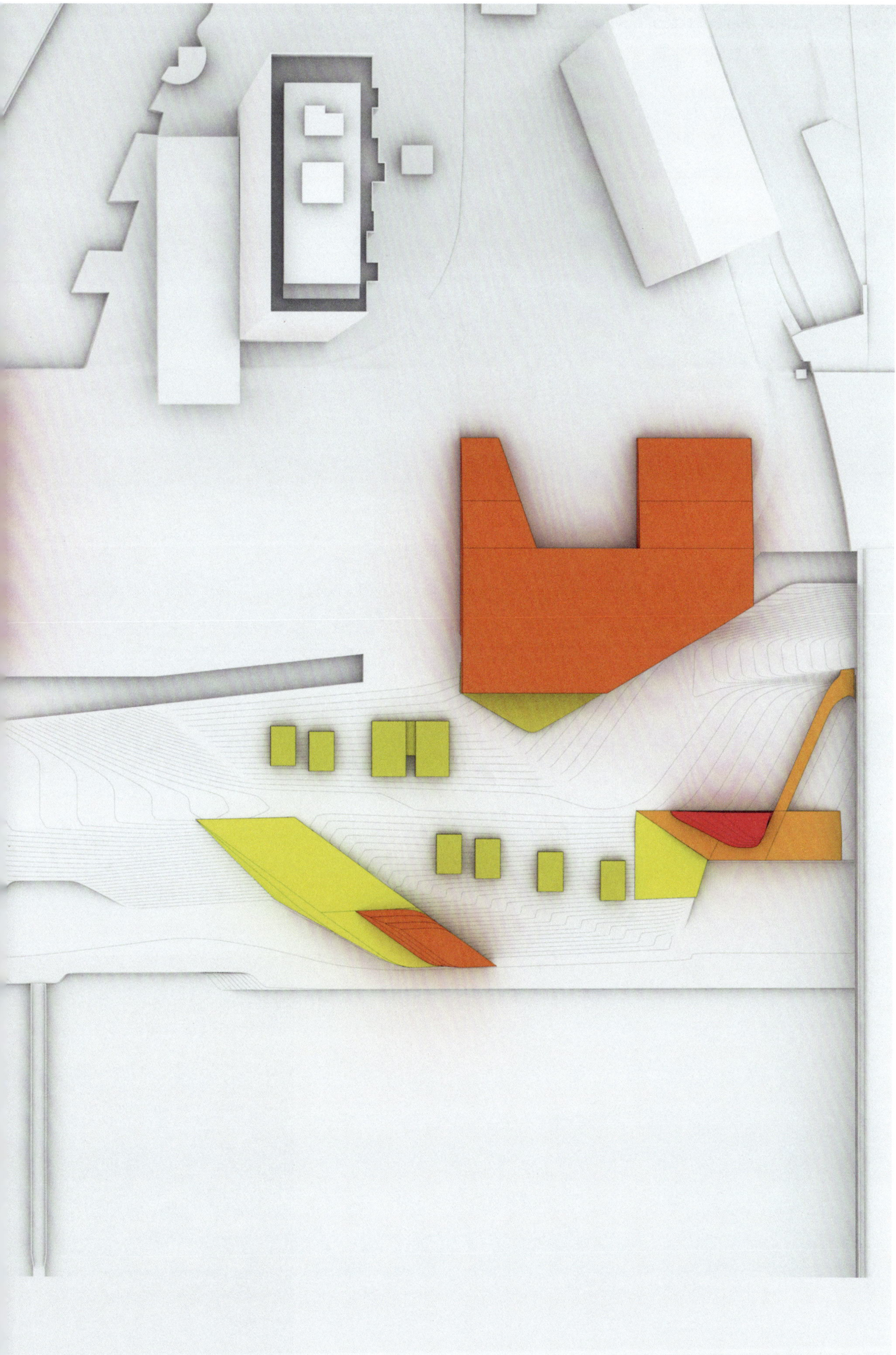

Zoning according to flood levels

Zonierung nach Hochwasserpegeln

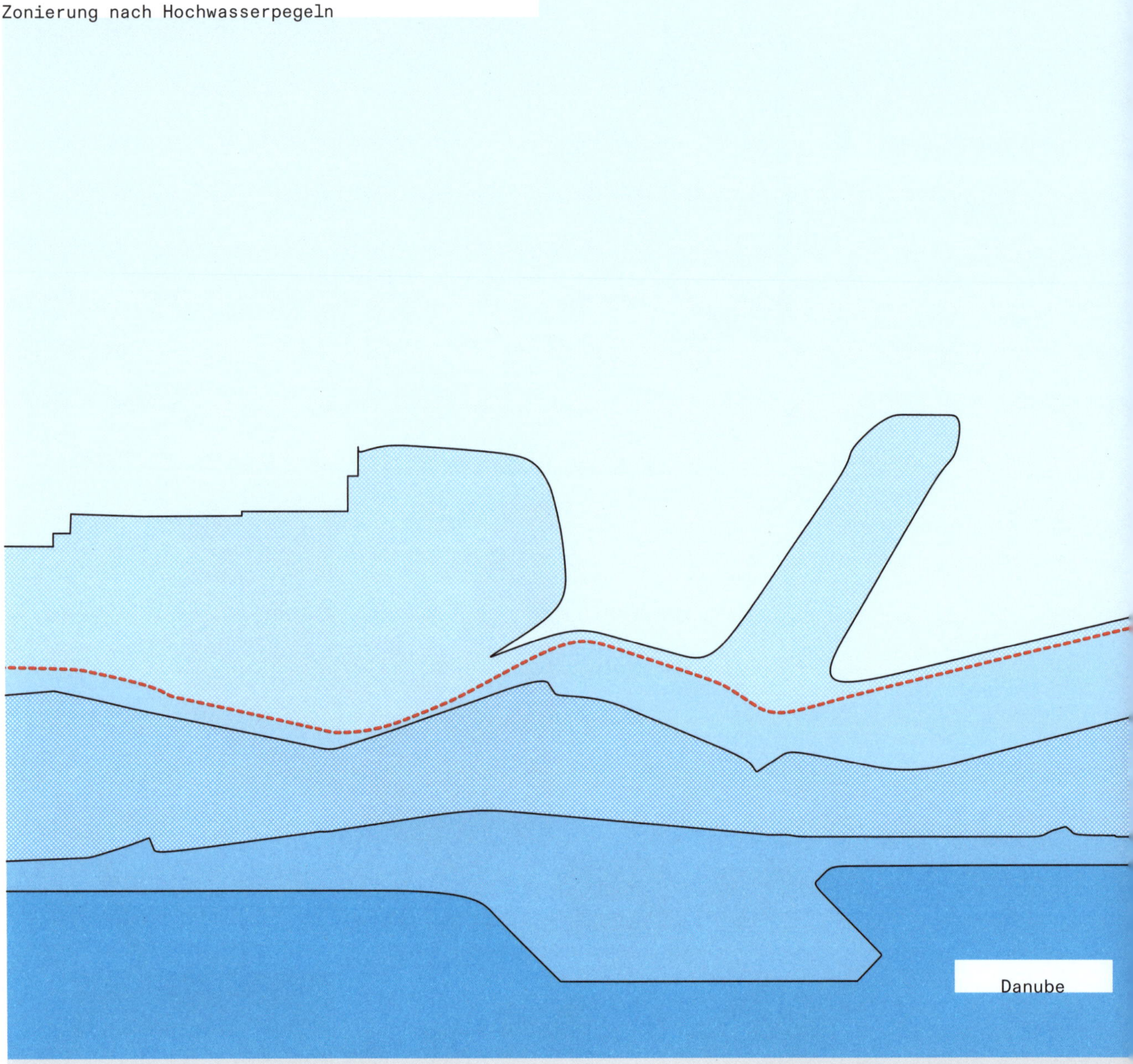

The New Danube was built on the occasion of the second Vienna Danube regulation from 1972 to 1987 as a spillway for flood protection. The flood protection system of the Danube area in Vienna is designed for a 1000-year flood. The floods of the last years reached a level of about 5.30 m above Vienna zero. This means that the Kaipromenade was flooded by about 3.10 m. According to the information of the Wiener Gewässer Management, the contour line or the freeboard, which ensures a permanent use, runs at 8.20 m above Vienna zero.

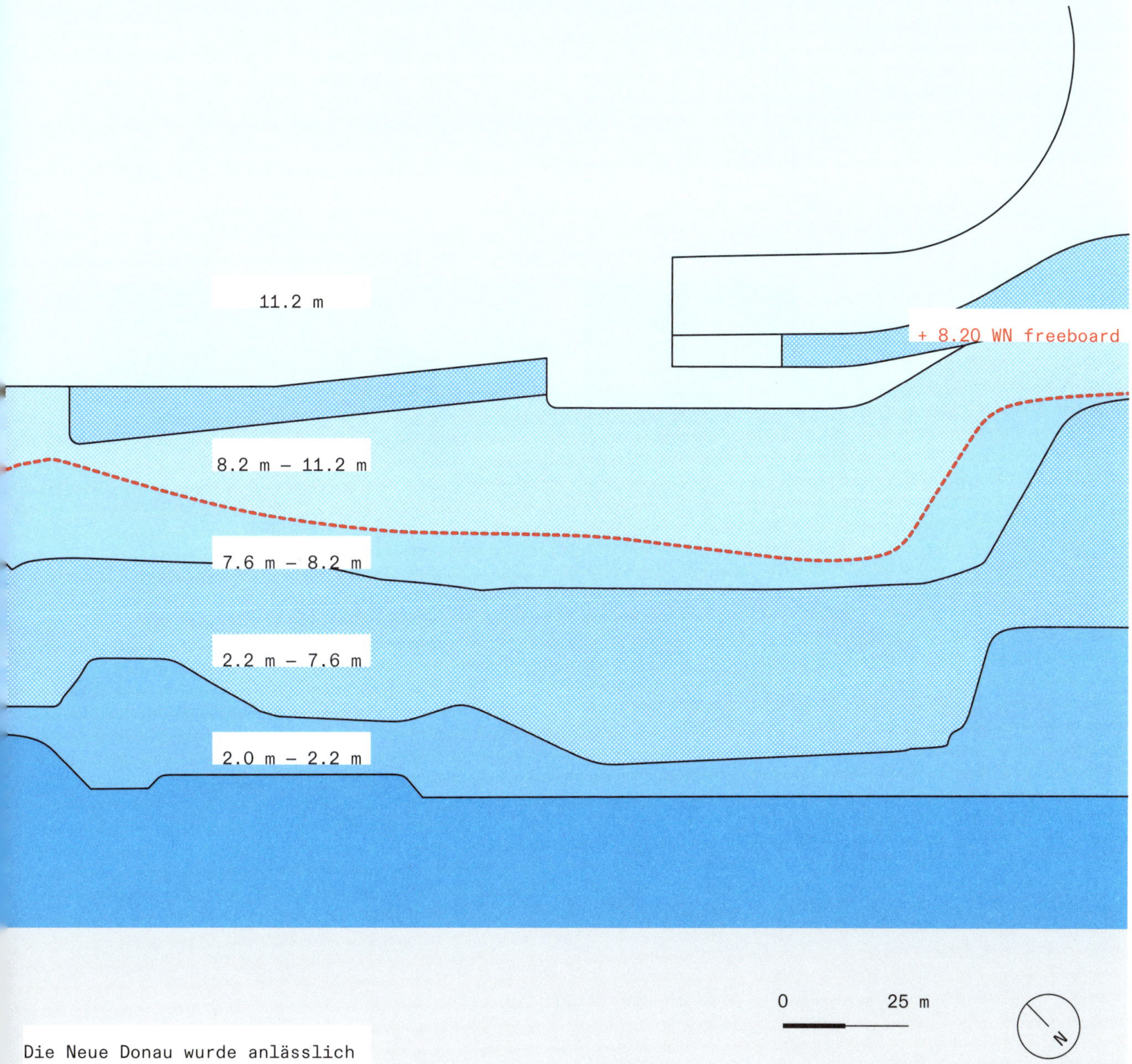

Die Neue Donau wurde anlässlich der zweiten Wiener Donauregulierung von 1972 bis 1987 als Entlastungsgerinne der Donau zum Hochwasserschutz gebaut. Das Hochwasserschutzsystem des Donauraums in Wien ist für ein 1000-jährliches Hochwasser projektiert. Die Überschwemmungen der letzten Jahre erreichten ein Niveau von ca. 5,30 m über Wiener Null, wodurch die Kaipromenade um etwa 3,10 m überflutet wurde. Den Angaben des Wiener Gewässer Managements zufolge wird das geplante Freibord auf 8,20 m über Wiener Null eine dauerhafte Nutzung gewährleisten.

Topographical modification by shifting land mass

Topografische Veränderung durch Verlagerung der Landmasse

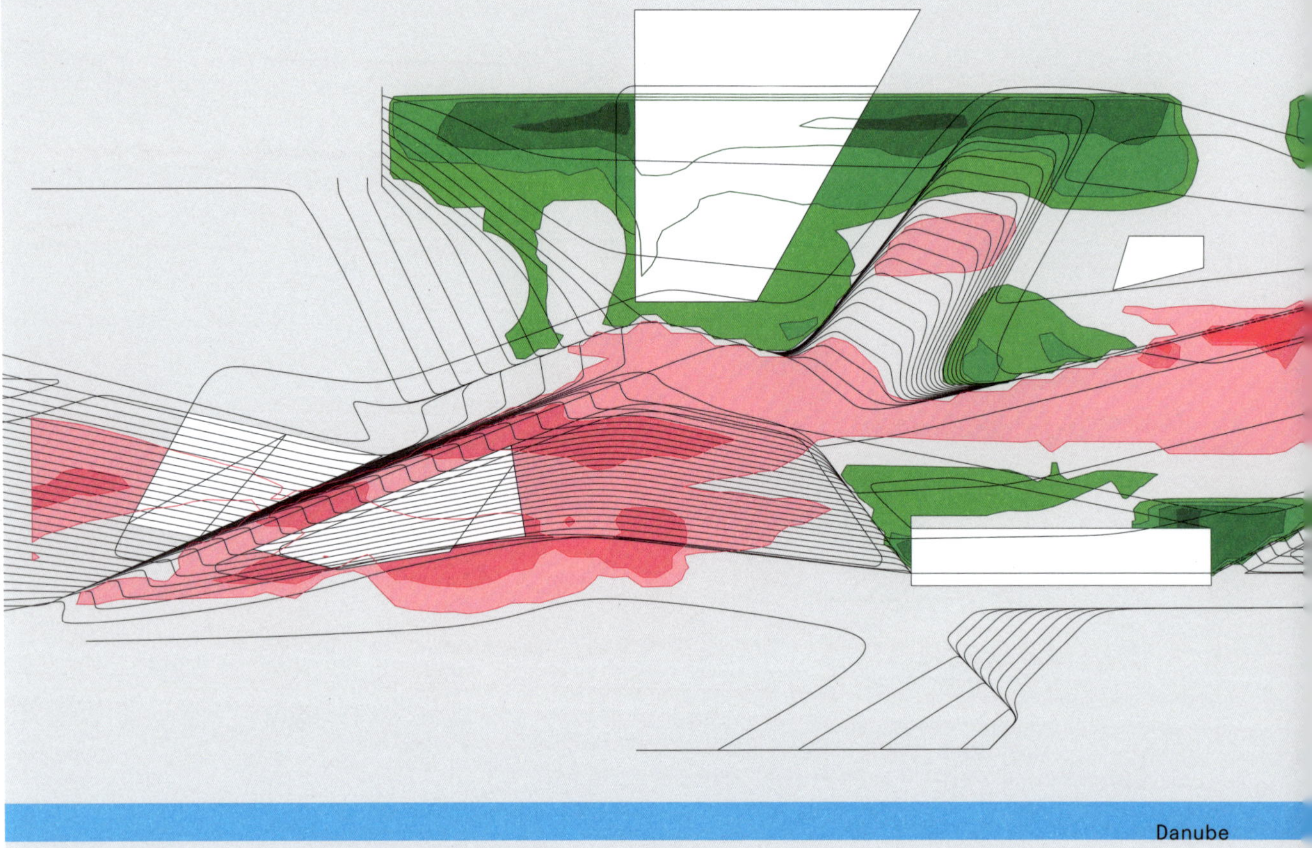

+ 1 m terrain fill Geländeauftrag

+ 2 m terrain fill Geländeauftrag

+ 3 m terrain fill Geländeauftrag

+ 4 m terrain fill Geländeauftrag

- 1 m terrain excavation Geländeabtrag

- 2 m terrain excavation Geländeabtrag

- 3 m terrain excavation Geländeabtrag

- 4 m terrain excavation Geländeabtrag

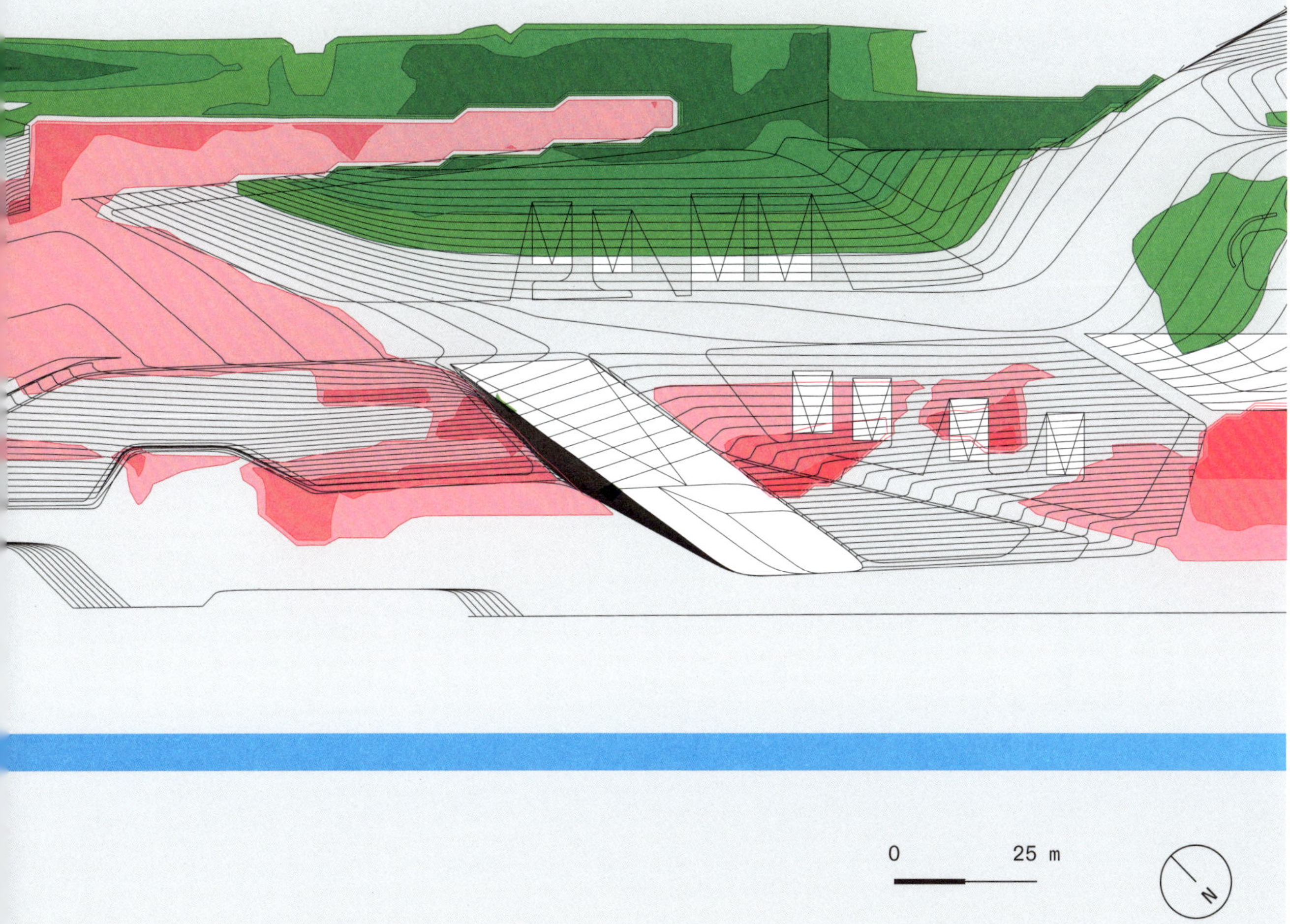

The obstacle is not only a welcome barrier for skaters, but a resistant figure in the hegemonic space.

Das Obstacle ist nicht nur eine willkommene Barriere für Skater, sondern auch eine widerständige Figur im hegemonialen Raum.

mix
22.3.
mix
22.3.
mix
CALMHAUS

mehr wien zum leben.
wienholding
mehr wien zum leben.
wienholding

SEEING THROUGH CLOUDS

Kathrin Aste

The desire to develop a form on the basis of contextually relevant information demands that this information is procured in many different ways. In addition to the classic research methods that shape the process of architectural design, we also use terrestrial laser scanning as a means of identifying the hidden qualities of a place.

Terrestrial laser scanning is a 3D imaging process that automatically records laser-based measurements of distance as a means of creating a geometrical model of a landscape, a building or an object. In contrast with standard measurement methods, the laser scanner records the object not as a series of individual representative points but, rather, as a multitude of points. These are described as a point cloud, which is initially white but can also be furnished with colour information via an integrated camera, in order to improve the visual quality of the digital model.

This translucent point cloud is an interesting medium for broadening spatial perception. It facilitates a new, deeper perspective and can clarify spatial and locational relationships as a means of offering us a more holistic image of tectonic, compositional and topological qualities.

The representation of an object as a point cloud creates a permeable space, a positive space, which appears infused with negative space.

The description of this negative space by the media scientist and art psychologist Rudolf Arnheim as the space that surrounds objects and, in the final analysis, models and illuminates the body[1] seems particularly appropriate for the point cloud, given the way in which this depicts space against a dark background that, like nocturnal space, lends it a balanced, atmospheric appearance.[2]

In this way, the point cloud provides us with information about not only the geometry and location of an object but also its immeasurable qualities. And, in doing so, it underlines the way in which atmospheres are also inherent elements of architecture.

Hence, the topology of the point cloud is not only the basis of a geometrical form but also a means of illustrating auratic qualities. This visualisation enables us to research all those spatial qualities of a place that go beyond its tangible morphological and physical state.

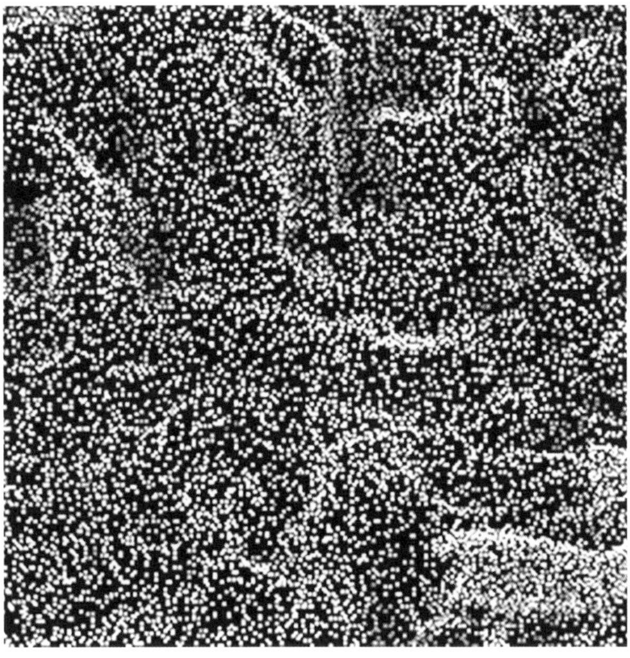

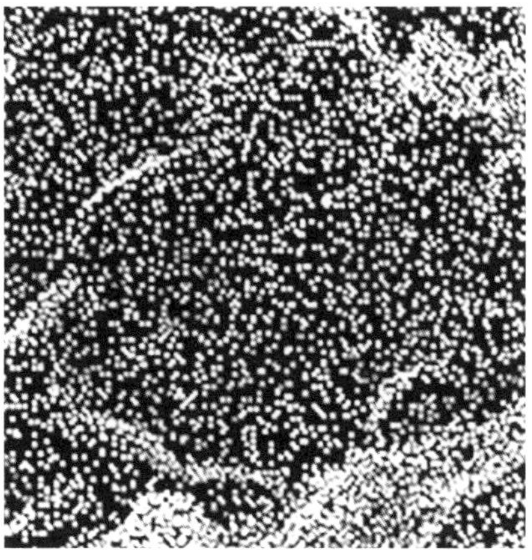

Das Bestreben, eine Form auf Basis kontextuell relevanter Informationen zu entwickeln, bedarf unterschiedlichster Methoden der Informationsbeschaffung. Neben diversen klassischen Arten des Recherchierens, die den architektonischen Entwurfsprozess prägen, verwenden wir den terrestrischen Laserscan, um verborgene Qualitäten eines Ortes zu erheben.

Der terrestrische Laserscan ist ein bildgebendes 3D-Verfahren, das laserbasierte Streckenmessungen automatisiert erfasst und daraus ein geometrisches Modell einer Landschaft, eines Bauwerks oder eines Objekts erstellt. Im Gegensatz zu herkömmlichen Vermessungsmethoden erfasst der Laserscanner das Objekt nicht anhand einzelner repräsentativer Punkte, sondern durch eine Vielzahl von Punkten. Diese Ansammlung an Punkten bezeichnet man als Punktwolke, die, ursprünglich weiß, zusätzlich mittels einer integrierten Kamera mit Farbinformation versehen wird, um die visuelle Qualität des digitalen Modells zu steigern.

Die transluzente Punktwolke ist ein interessantes Medium zur Erweiterung der Raumwahrnehmung. Sie ermöglicht einen anderen, tieferen Blick und kann Raum- und Lagebeziehungen verdeutlichen. Tektonische, kompositorische und topologische Beschaffenheiten werden dadurch ganzheitlicher sichtbar.

Durch die Darstellung eines Objektes als Punktwolke entsteht ein durchlässiger Raum, ein Positiv-Raum, der vom Negativ-Raum durchdrungen scheint.

Die Beschreibung des Negativ-Raums seitens Medienwissenschaftler und Kunstpsychologe Rudolf Arnheim als Raum, der die Dinge umgibt, der letztlich den Körper modelliert und beleuchtet, scheint auf die Punktwolke besonders zuzutreffen,[1] da sie den Raum wie den Nachtraum auf schwarzem Hintergrund darstellt und ihm eine gestimmte, atmosphärische Wirkung verleiht.[2]

Für unsere Arbeit erhalten wir durch die Punktwolke also Auskunft sowohl über die Geometrie und Lage eines Objekts als auch über seine unmessbaren Qualitäten; und es wird offensichtlich, dass Atmosphären inhärente Elemente der Architektur sind.

Die Topologie der Punktwolke ist somit nicht nur Grundlage eines geometrischen Gebildes, sondern verdeutlicht auratische Qualitäten. Diese Visualisierung ermöglicht es uns, jene Eigenschaften von Raum zu erforschen, die über den visualisierten morphologischen und physischen Zustand eines Ortes hinausgehen.

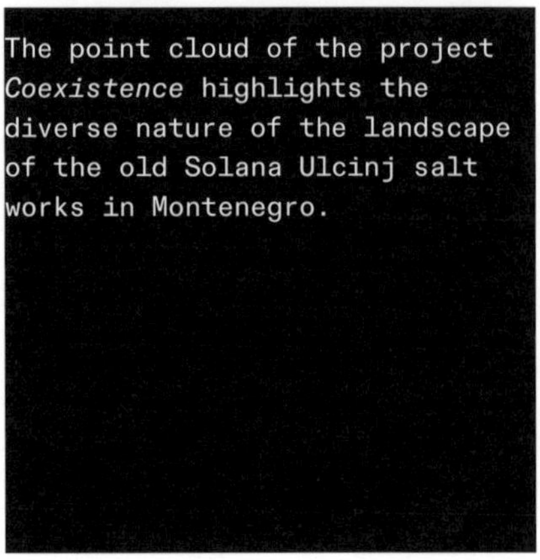

The point cloud of the project *Coexistence* highlights the diverse nature of the landscape of the old Solana Ulcinj salt works in Montenegro.

1 Rudolf Arnheim, *To the Rescue of Art: Twenty-Six Essays*, Berkeley / Los Angeles 1992, p. 92, c.f. the video documentation of the public lecture *Der negative Raum, Teil 1* by Peter Weibel at the Institute for Spatial Experiments (Professor Olafur Eliasson), Berlin University of the Arts, 8 May 2009, http://www.raumexperimente.net/de/single/peter-weibel-the-negative-space-part-i/ [06.08.2013], c.f. Martina Tritthart, "Der negative Raum oder die andere Seite des Lichts. Maria Nordman and Nan Hoover: Wahrnehmung Raum Kunst Architektur", in: *ALL-OVER*, no. 5, autumn 2013, http://allo-ver-magazin.com/?p=1557.

2 Otto Friedrich Bollnow, *Mensch und Raum*, Stuttgart 1963, c.f. Martina Tritthart, "Der negative Raum oder die andere Seite des Lichts. Maria Nordman and Nan Hoover: Wahrnehmung Raum Kunst Architektur", in: *ALL-OVER*, no. 5, autumn 2013, http://allo-ver-magazin.com/?p=1557.

Die Punktwolke im Projekt *Coexistence* beleuchtet die diverse Beschaffenheit der Landschaft des alten Salzwerkes Solana Ulcinj in Montenegro.

A PARADIGM FOR COEXISTENCE

Marco Russo

We are venturing elsewhere without ever having made a step in this direction and we are diving into an unknown dimension made of noise that turns into a visual experience.

A multitude of points, point by point, once slacked and once ranked, scattered in the vastness, a synchronised generation of compression and resolution into thousandfold. All these elements are visualising a landscape in which well-known forms of accumulation are converging into a geometry of new structures.

fog dust agglomeration

The territory that we are prospecting is made by pulsating and dynamic elements. The landscape is going to unleash its own wasteland and mutates itself to a universe and to a medium of a new cosmology:

expansion fluctuation acceleration
centre and periphery
singularity and multitude

If the virtual is handled as a pure fiction, a phantasm or a ghost, the virtual appears as something not concrete. It appears as a mysterious entity, something abstract beyond the concreteness of experienced realm.

However, if virtuality is handled as a strategy of communication, the virtual room appears as the expansion of being and at least as the expansion of the concrete – then what is virtual is the real that is just as yet unrealised.

Playing and experimenting with virtual rooms is at least an expression of a primordial and intimate human instinct. It is an instinct that motivates us to design utopias managing the future as a realisable occurrence of the contemporary. Utopias and virtuality are not non-places or fictional spaces but forces of exploration.

The virtual room is a speculative room. It is the poetic ability to take a glance from the future to our past and realising that this past is now.

The morphology of the point cloud is agglomeration of algorithms. The point cloud is a medium of information, legibility and narration. The point cloud is also a paradigm for coexistence in which the gradually sized takes place at the same time as their own possibility without interference of one element from another.

Coexistence implies the simultaneous occurrence and presence of different elements, such as creature, species and systems at a specific location. This concept shows how existence and topos belong together and are mutually dependent. Both elements are inevitably linked to a spatiotemporal dimension. Everything that exists has a duration and is due to its presence both a spatial intervention and expansion. However, the term "coexistence" means a particular form of existence. Coexistence is the form of existence in which multiplicity becomes one unit and where the individual has no territorial claim towards the collective. If a place is characterised by coexistence, it is not a territory anymore.

The Solana Ulcinj is not a territory, it is a landscape which is characterised by coexistence and diversity. The biodiversity of the Solana is the result of a converting process. Environmental change is determined by specific social, cultural, political or economic conditions and the institutions that accompany them. The process of socio-environmental metabolic circulations transforms both social and physical environments and produces social and physical milieux with new and distinctive qualities.

Solana Ulcinj is a place of narrations. It is a narration of an area and its related fates. For this, Solana Ulcinj is not only a singular space but a symbol for other places worldwide with a similar story and reveals at the same time the entanglement of the global into the local. This anti-territorial and virtual experiment would give new inputs for new ways of abstraction.

In that sense the Solana Ulcinj is an example of the blurring boundary between the natural and the artificial and it emphasises the landscape as a composition of nature elements and as a socio-cultural idea. It invites us to perceive the qualities of this unified structure within which the coexistence of natural and artificial systems created a specific environment.

The Solana Ulcinj is a narrative interrelation between utopia and tragedy, between reality and fiction that encourages its exploration.

(Audio document / Audiodokument)

Marco Russo is a philosopher working at the intersection of philosophy, art and music. He is the manager of the col legno music label. He writes texts, gives lectures and teaches at the Faculty of Architecture in Innsbruck, among other places. Furthermore he is co-creator of artistic actions at columbosnext and Verschubu Records.

Marco Russo ist Philosoph und arbeitet an der Schnittstelle zwischen Philosophie, Kunst und Musik. Er ist als Manager des Labels col legno Music tätig. Er verfasst Texte, hält Vorträge und unterrichtet u.a. an der Fakultät für Architektur in Innsbruck. Außerdem ist er Mitgestalter von künstlerischen Aktionen bei columbosnext und Verschubu Records.

Coexistence was exhibited in the Montenegro Pavilion at the 15th International Architecture Biennale in Venice in 2016.

Curated by Bart Lootsma und Katharina Weinberger

Coexistence wurde 2016 im montenegrinischen Pavillon auf der 15. Internationalen Architekturbiennale in Venedig ausgestellt.

Kuratiert von Bart Lootsma und Katharina Weinberger

VAB	Sphäre 1:50.000	2018	Architecture Biennale	Venice Italy

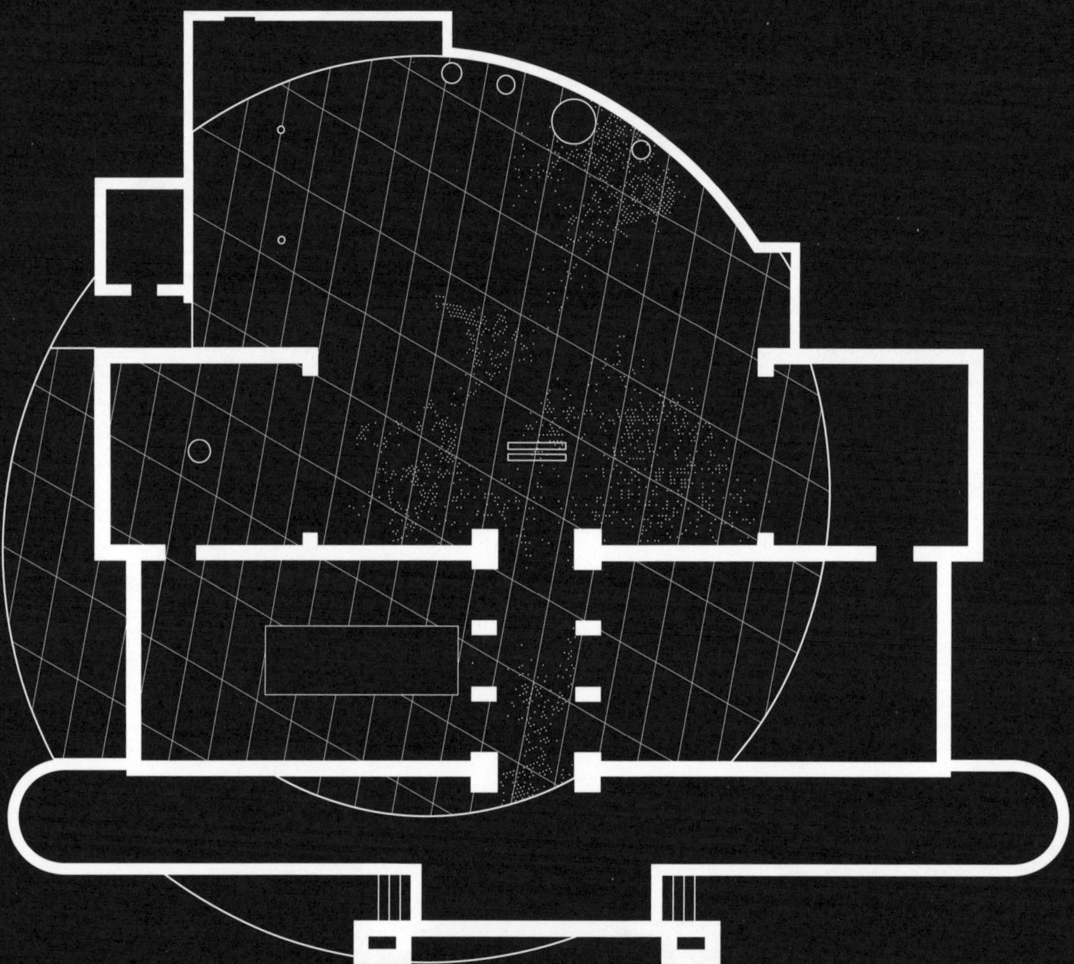

PROJECT	TITLE	YEAR	SUBJECT	LOCATION

The Austrian Pavilion is essentially perceived as a strictly symmetrical building. It was built in 1934 according to a design by Josef Hoffmann and Robert Kramreiter. Twenty years later, two years before his death, Hoffmann added a curved garden wall. This gesture can be seen as one of deviation, as a revolutionising of one's own design, as a transition from an absolute to a relative understanding of space.

An apparently Euclidian circular surface was inscribed in the floor of the pavilion in a geometrical reference to the curved form of the garden wall. The curvature of this surface makes it clear that it is the manifestation of the segment of a sphere. The suggested spherical volume decentralises the building, diminishing the dominance of its axes.

Whether as a result of the use of the golden section in the historical design or, simply, of pure chance, the sphere in the Austrian Pavilion has a radius of 128 metres and, hence, a scale of 1:50,000 vis-à-vis the earth. Like the earth itself, the curved surface is a volume. A volume in the ground, whose reflective surface tells of the duality of the space and questions our relationship with our planet. It illustrates a space in which one sees oneself where one is not and brings to mind the space in which one is actually situated. It bends, distorts, transports and facilitates a leap to another scale, to another place that is beyond the given and the imaginable. In this way, the mirror becomes an instrument of deviation rather than of symmetry. Symmetry and deviation confront each other and reciprocate, expanding the spaces of the pavilion.

Der Österreichische Pavillon wird vorwiegend als streng symmetrisches Gebäude wahrgenommen. Er wurde 1934 nach Entwürfen von Josef Hoffmann und Robert Kramreiter errichtet. 20 Jahre später, zwei Jahre vor seinem Tod, fügte Josef Hoffmann eine bogenförmige Gartenmauer hinzu. Diese Geste kann als Abweichung gedeutet werden, als Revolutionieren des eigenen Entwurfs, als Übergang von einem absoluten Raumverständnis hin zu einem relativen.

Geometrisch bezugnehmend auf die Bogenform der Gartenmauer, wurde in den Pavillon eine scheinbar euklidische Kreisfläche eingeschrieben. Durch die Krümmung dieser Fläche wird deutlich, dass sich an der Oberfläche das Segment einer Sphäre offenbart. Der angedeutete, kugelförmige Körper dezentralisiert das Bauwerk und rückt es aus seiner strengen Axialität.

Sei es nun eine Folge der Anwendung des goldenen Schnitts im historischen Entwurf oder einfach purer Zufall, die Sphäre im Österreichischen Pavillon misst einen Radius von 128 Metern und steht somit im Verhältnis von 1:50.000 zur Erde. Die gekrümmte Fläche ist wie die Erde selbst ein Körper. Ein Boden-Körper, dessen verspiegelte Oberfläche von der Dualität des Raums erzählt und unser Verhältnis zur Erde hinterfragt. Sie veranschaulicht einen Raum, in dem man sich sieht, wo man nicht ist, und vergegenwärtigt jenen Ort, an dem man sich befindet. Sie krümmt, verzerrt, transloziert und ermöglicht einen maßstäblichen Sprung, einen Sprung in ein Außen, in ein Außerhalb des Gegebenen und Vorstellbaren.

The surface of the sphere is vulnerable. It is not only reflective in the sense of visual effect but also reactive, through its materiality, to atmospheric influences such as light, temperature and rain. The resulting spatial image is not static but, rather, one that emerges through its interaction with the context. This is an oppositional space. A vulnerable, hot and cold space, soiled and scratched. A space, whose transcendence opposes any conventional function and, through precisely this opposition, underlines its social purpose. Thus, the inscribed sphere creates a new context. A new spatial configuration that does away with outside and inside, above and below, here and there. The result is a synthesis that is based on the recognition of the complex, the ambivalent, the unstable and the fragmentary. This is an understanding of space that establishes a relationship between place and identity, form and materiality. *Sphäre 1:50,000* is a poetic mise-en-scène, a spatial deviation.

So wird der Spiegel zum Instrument der Abweichung anstatt der Symmetrie. Symmetrie und Abweichung stehen einander wechselseitig gegenüber und erweitern die Räume des Pavillons.

Die Oberfläche der Sphäre ist eine verletzliche. Sie ist nicht nur reflektierend im Sinne optischer Wirksamkeit, sondern reagiert auch in ihrer Materialität auf atmosphärische Einflüsse wie Licht, Temperatur und Regen. Somit wird kein statisches Bild von Raum gezeichnet, sondern eines, das aus der Wechselwirkung mit der Umwelt resultiert. Es entsteht ein gegensätzlicher Raum. Ein verletzbarer, heißer und kalter Raum, der verschmutzt und zerkratzt. Ein Raum, der sich in seiner Übersteigerung jeglicher herkömmlichen Funktion widersetzt und gerade darin seine gesellschaftliche Funktion unterstreicht. Die eingeschriebene Sphäre schafft so einen neuen Kontext. Eine neue räumliche Konfiguration, die das Außen, Innen, Oben, Unten, Da und Dort auflöst. Die Folge ist eine Synthese, basierend auf der Anerkennung des Komplexen, Ambivalenten, Unbeständigen und Fragmentarischen. Durch dieses Verständnis von Raum werden Ort und Identität, Form und Materialität in Relation gebracht. *Sphäre 1:50.000* ist eine poetische Inszenierung, eine räumliche Abweichung.

The exhibition *Thoughts Form Matter* presented three spatial installations, in the context of the 16th International Architecture Biennale in Venice 2018. *Sphäre 1:50.000* approaches the topic of freespace by means of a spatial deviation that tells of multilayered spatial relationships.

Curated by Verena Konrad

Die Ausstellung *Thoughts Form Matter* präsentierte im Rahmen der 16. Internationalen Architekturbiennale in Venedig 2018 drei Rauminstallationen. *Sphäre 1:50.000* näherte sich dem Thema des Freiraums durch eine räumliche Abweichung, die von vielschichtigen räumlichen Beziehungen erzählt.

Kuratiert von Verena Konrad

LHP	Landhaus- platz	2010	Public square	Innsbruck Austria

The historical circumstances and period in which a building is built cannot be compared with the effect caused by a project and the way in which it influences a place and time. In a similar way to natural forms, architectural forms trigger actions and reactions. But only a spatial transformation and interpretation of a place leads to change and new possibilities.

"[...] in fact, it is the constraints of the architecture, its formal particularity and persistence beyond any functionalist determination, that truly embodies freedom. For in being neither uniformly open nor uniformly closed, it lies open to the unforeseen as it works on our changing activities over time." This understanding of architecture is advocated by Reiser and Umemoto in the introduction to their *Atlas of Novel Tectonics* as a way of describing the basic approach to designing a public square.

The objective of the remodelling of Landhausplatz was to realise a modern urban public space that interacts within the contradictory circumstances of the place and its wider context. Today, the square is home to a colourful mix of urban activities, a transformative basis for a range of protagonists from skaters to historic monuments. The new square reinforces the role of these monuments as witnesses, clarifies attitudes towards them and invites critical reflection on the history of the province.

A topography of gentle mounds stretches across the square, creating a richly landscaped counterpoint to the surrounding buildings. At the same time, however, the urban context of the topography, combined with its materialisation and function, transforms the ensemble into an urban sculpture that is both a square and a route. It presents itself as a body with a haptically highly active surface, whose texture switches from rough to highly polished in a series of partly flowing and partly abrupt transitions determined by its changing functions. The result is a broad variety of usable open-air elements such as mounds, fountains, plinths of monuments and seats that are arranged below and between the many groups of trees.

Die historischen Umstände und die Zeit, in der ein Bauwerk entsteht, sind nicht gleichzusetzen mit dem Effekt, den ein Projekt auslöst, und wie es einen Ort und seine Zeit beeinflusst. Ähnlich wie bei natürlichen Systemen löst die Gestalt der Architektur Aktionen und Reaktionen aus. Erst eine räumliche Transformation und Interpretation eines Ortes schaffen Veränderungen und neue Möglichkeiten.

„[...], denn in der Tat sind es die Zwänge der Architektur und deren formale Besonderheit und Persistenz jenseits jeder funktionalistischen Bestimmung, welche die Freiheit verkörpern. Denn da sie weder gänzlich bestimmt noch gänzlich unbestimmt ist, ist sie offen für das Unvorhergesehene und verändert sich im Wandel der Benützung." Dieses Verständnis von Architektur vertreten Reiser und Umemoto in der Einführung ihres *Atlas of Novel Tectonics* und beschreiben damit die Grundhaltung des Platzentwurfes.

Das Ziel der Neugestaltung des Landhausplatzes war es, einen modernen urbanen öffentlichen Raum zu realisieren, der innerhalb der widersprüchlichen Bedingungen des Ortes und seiner Umgebung interagiert. Heute ist der Platz ein Terrain für eine bunte Mischung urbaner Aktivitäten, eine transformative Basis für diverse Protagonist*innen von Skater*innen bis zum Denkmal. Der neue Platz stärkt die Denkmäler vor Ort in ihrer Funktion als Zeitzeugen, klärt deren Rezeptionen und ermöglicht eine kritische Reflexion der Geschichte des Landes.

Eine Topografie sanfter Hügel erstreckt sich über den Platz und setzt bildhaft einen landschaftsartigen Gegenpol zur Umgebung. Gleichzeitig aber wird die Topografie im städtischen Kontext durch ihre Materialisierung und Funktion zu einer urbanen Plastik, die gleichzeitig Platz und Weg ist. Diese zeigt sich als Körper mit haptisch hochaktiver Oberfläche, deren Textur in teils fließenden, teils abrupten Übergängen je nach Nutzungsanforderung von rau bis zu hochglanzpoliert wechselt. So entstehen vielfältig nutzbare Freiflächen, wie Hügel, Brunnen, Podeste für Denkmäler oder Sitzgelegenheiten unter und zwischen den zahlreichen Baumgruppen.

The demolition of the old plaza above the ceiling of the existing underground parking garage unmasks the site and begins to tell its story.

Der Abriss des alten Platzes über der Decke der bestehenden Tiefgarage entlarvt den Ort und beginnt, seine Geschichte zu erzählen.

LANDHAUS

Sixteen questions / One deductive process

Sechzehn Fragen / Eine Ableitung

What do we think about when we look at the monuments?

Woran denken wir beim Betrachten der Denkmäler?

Is this two squares or one?

Sind es zwei Plätze oder einer?

Do some people avoid the square?

Wird der Platz gemieden?

Is there anyone who should remain outside?

Soll irgendjemand draußen bleiben?

Is the clarification of the setting between the Franzosendenkmal and the Landhaus a second project?

Ist die Klärung der Situation zwischen Franzosendenkmal und Landhaus ein zweites Projekt?

Can form, manner of execution and positioning be read on a meta-level as symbols of a culture of reception and a mission to represent?

Können Form, Art der Ausführung und Platzierung auf einer Metaebene als Zeichen von Rezeptionskultur und Repräsentationsauftrag gelesen werden?

Can a poetic, metaphysical urban base be created by incorporating pebbles from the river Sill and the river Inn?

Kann durch das Einfließen von Kiesel aus Sill und Inn eine poetische, metaphysische urbane Basis geschaffen werden?

"A cherished urban green space" vis-à-vis the surrounding Alpine pastures and functioning urban parks, gardens and oases?

„Wertvoller innerstädtischer Grünraum" angesichts der alpinen Matten ringsum und funktionierender innerstädtischer Parks, Gärten, Oasen?

Should a new work of art take a communicating, commenting position?

Soll ein neues Kunstwerk kommunizierend, kommentierend Platz nehmen?

Should grass grow on the square?

Soll Gras über den Platz wachsen?

Are there any misunderstandings?

Gibt es Missverständnisse?

"Space comes from spacing, clearing out" (M. Heidegger)

„Raum kommt von räumen, roden"
(M. Heidegger)

Do they contribute to the historical image?

Leisten sie einen Beitrag zum Geschichtsbild?

How do new visual axes come about?

Wie entstehen neue Blickachsen?

Can interventions enable us to experience distance and proximity in a new way?

Können Interventionen neue Erfahrungen von Distanz und Nähe erreichen?

Body or surface?

Körper oder Fläche?

Can the monuments be brought into the present?

Können die Denkmäler in die Gegenwart geholt werden?

Decision of the BDA Federal Monuments Office 04.06.2010
GZ: 47.680/2/2010 Ref: Innsbruck Eduard-Wallnöfer-Platz
Liberation Monument and Memorial 1363-1963

Ruling, Item 2
The steps of the Liberation Monument (Franzosendenkmal) are to be retained below the new concrete works.
A separating layer is to be laid in order to adequately protect the steps.

Bescheid BDA Bundesdenkmalamt 04.06.2010
GZ: 47.680/2/2010 Betreff: Innsbruck Eduard-Wallnöfer-Platz
Befreiungsdenkmal und Denkmal 1363-1963

Spruch Pkt.2
Die Stufen des Befreiungsdenkmales (Franzosendenkmales) sind unter der neuen Betonierung zur erhalten. Für ausreichenden Schutz der Stufen ist eine Trennschicht einzulegen.

First phase of competition

1. Stufe Wettbewerb

In July 1945, French troops replaced US forces as the occupying power in Tyrol. The Head of the French Military Government, General Administrator Pierre Voizard, proposed the construction of a monument in memory of the resistance shown by local people and of the Allied soldiers who had been killed in action.

Im Juli 1945 lösten die französischen Truppen die Streitkräfte der USA als Besatzungsmacht in Tirol ab. Der Chef der französischen Militärregierung, Generaladministrator Pierre Voizard, regte den Bau eines Denkmals an, das an den Widerstand Einheimischer und an die gefallenen alliierten Soldaten erinnern sollte.

GUIDELINES FOR THE USE OF EDUARD-WALLNÖFER-PLATZ (LANDHAUSPLATZ)

The Province of Tyrol warmly welcomes all users of Eduard-Wallnöfer-Platz.
This square invites visitors to rest awhile, take a stroll or engage in sport.
This is also a place where children can play.
Wherever many people are doing different things, some rules are always necessary.
This is why we would like to ask you, when performing your various functions and activities, to consider each other, to observe the points listed below and to use these facilities, which are the property of the Province of Tyrol, carefully and, hence, in the interests of all citizens.

I The road traffic regulations apply at all times.
1. Eduard-Wallnöfer-Platz can be used by all under the same conditions. This is why the road traffic regulations apply.
2. Motor vehicles are prohibited from using the entire Eduard-Wallnöfer-Platz, with the exception of emergency vehicles, motor vehicles that are obliged to arrive on or depart from the square on a case-by-case basis and government vehicles.

RICHTLINIEN ZUR BENÜTZUNG DES EDUARD-WALLNÖFER-PLATZES (LANDHAUSPLATZ)

Das Land Tirol heißt alle Benützer des Edunrd-Wallnöfor-Platzes herzlich willkommen.
Dieser Platz lädt ein zum Verweilen, Spazierengehen oder zur Sportausübung.
Ebenso finden Kinder hier Raum zum Spielen.
Wo viele Menschen unterschiedliche Dinge tun, geht es nicht ohne Regeln.
Daher bitten wir Sie, bei der Ausübung dieser Nutzungen und Tätigkeiten aufeinander Rücksicht zu nehmen, die unten angeführten Punkte zu beachten und die Anlage als Eigentum des Landes Tirol und damit im Interesse aller Bürgerinnen und Bürger schonend zu behandeln.

I Geltung der StVO
1. Der Eduard-Wallnöfer-Platz kann von allen unter den gleichen Bedingungen benützt werden. Es gilt daher die Straßenverkehrsordnung.
2. Am gesamten Eduard-Wallnöfer-Platz gilt ein Fahrverbot für Kraftfahrzeuge mit Ausnahme von Einsatzfahrzeugen oder von Kraftfahrzeugen für notwendige Zu- und Abfahrten im Einzelfall sowie von Regierungsfahrzeugen.

In cooperation with Stiefel Kramer Architecture and Christopher Grüner

3D mesh model

3D-Netzmodell

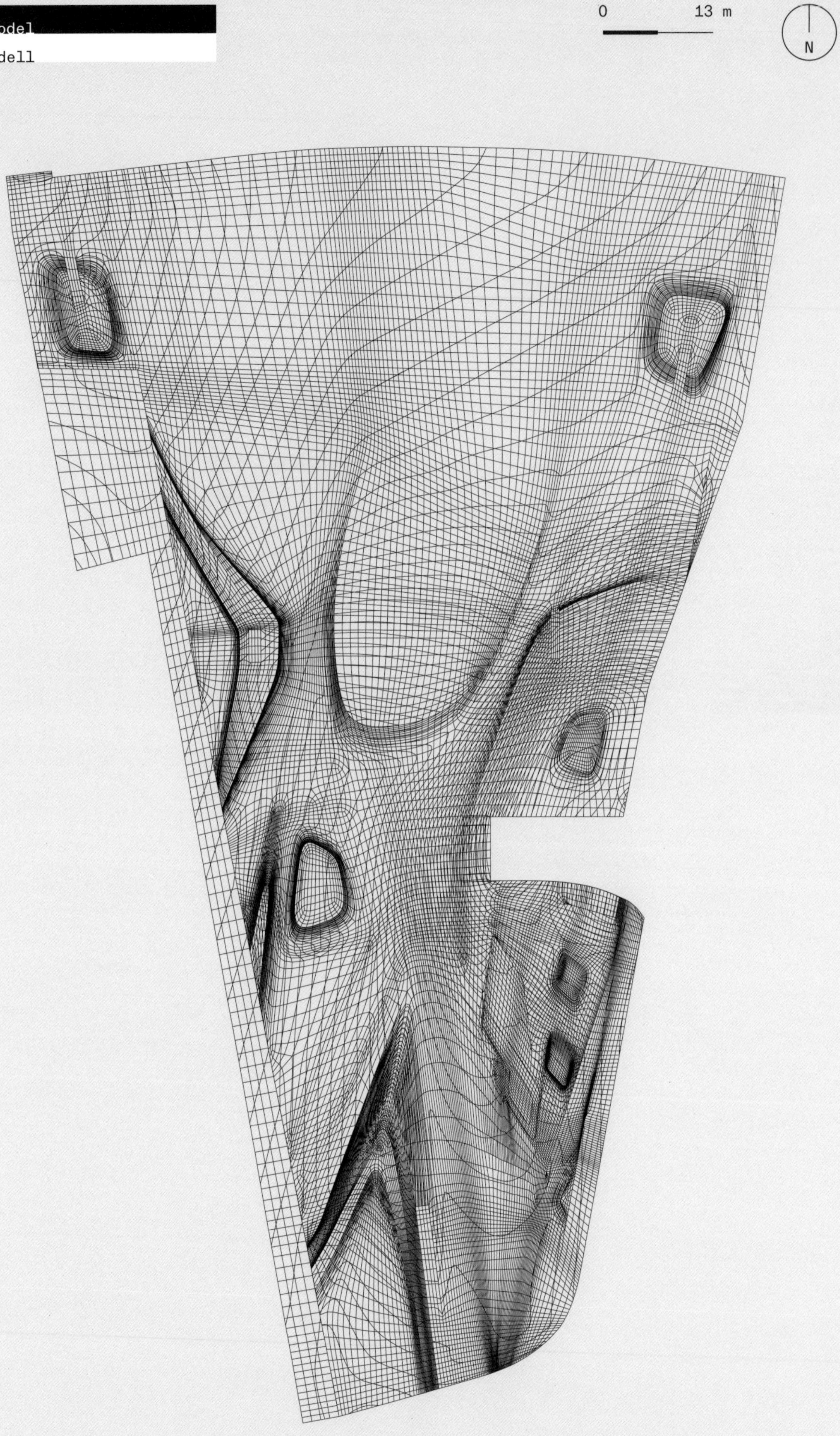

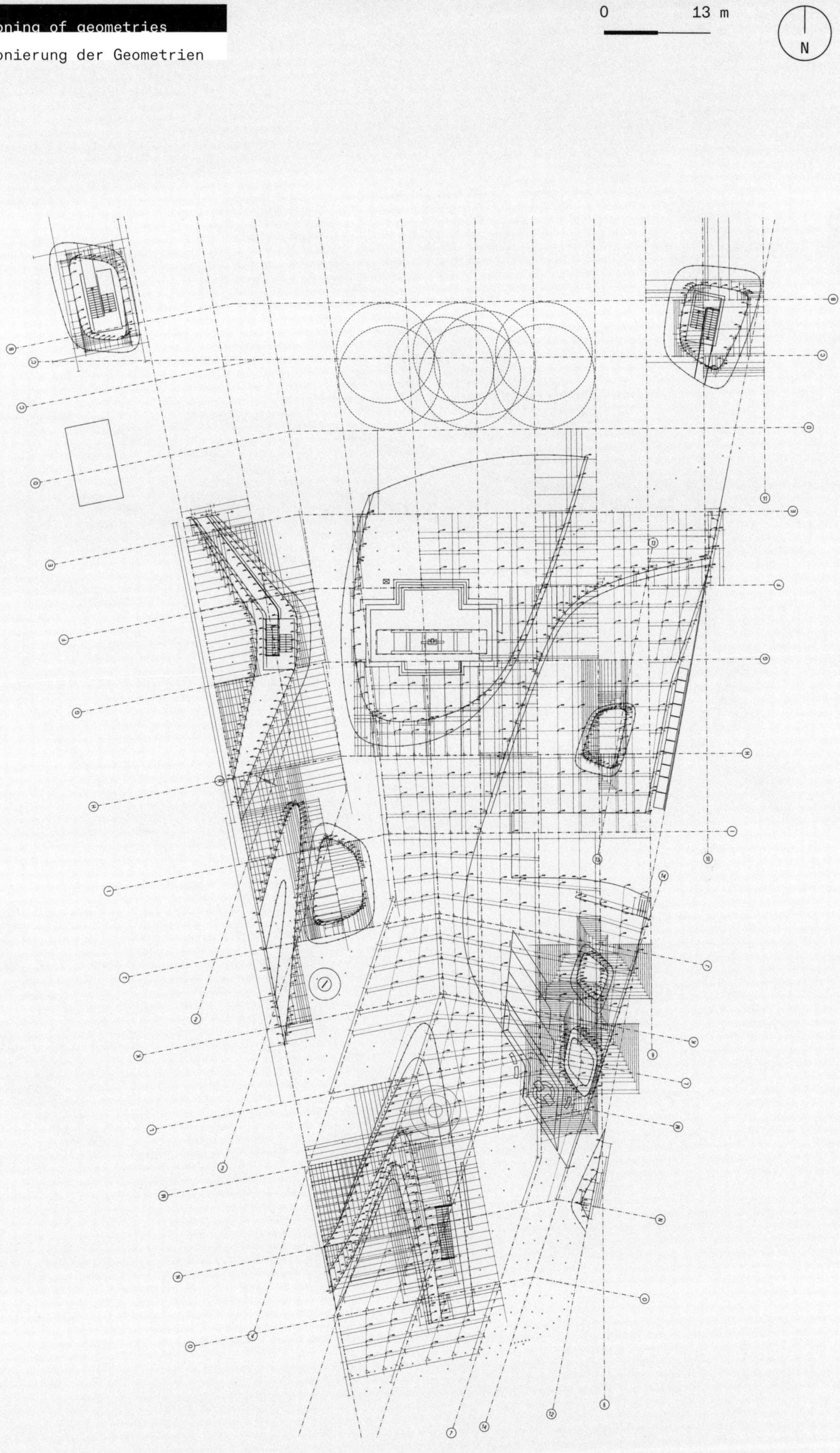
0
13 m
N

SWIETELSKY

pension series
EAST

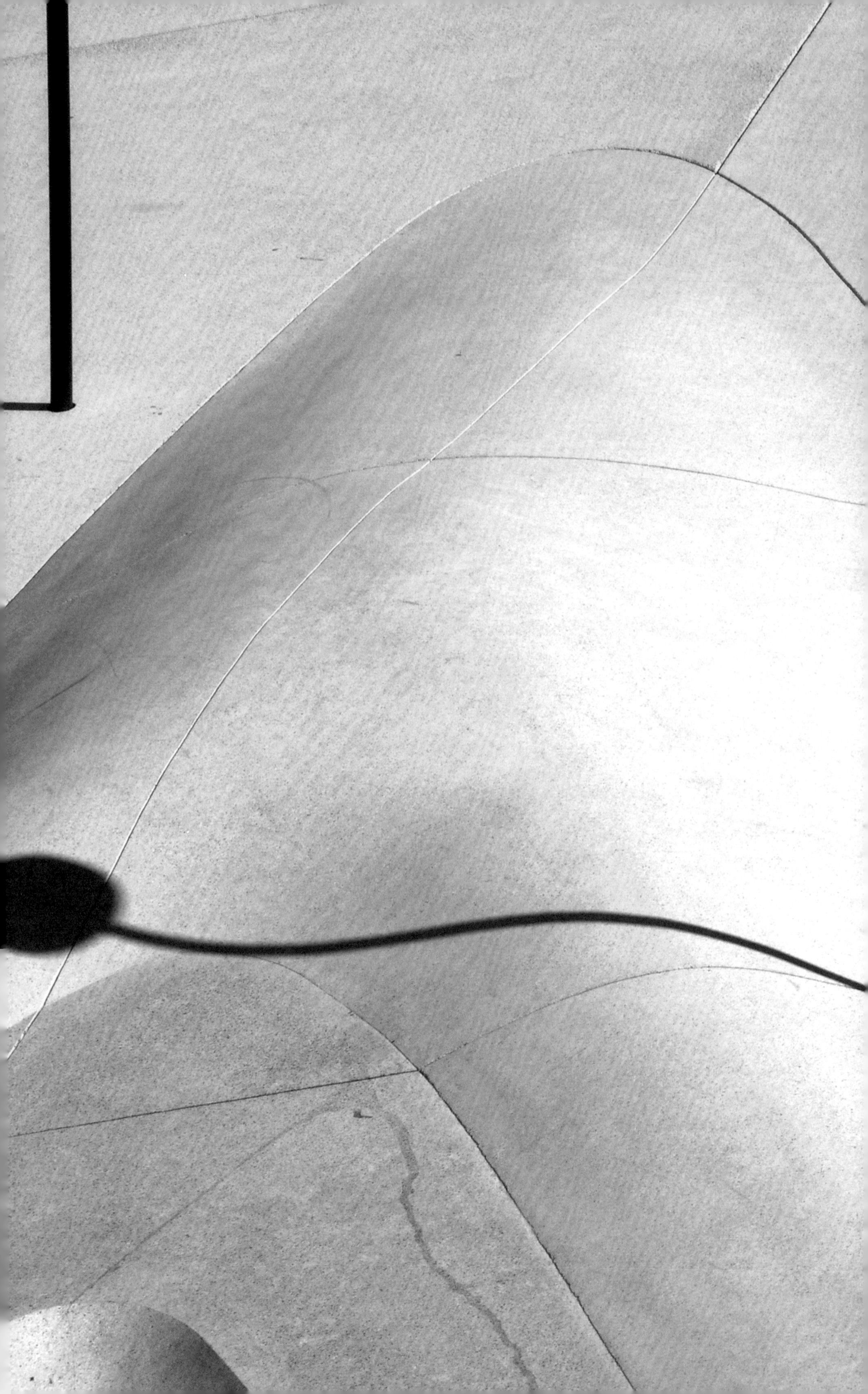

THE GROUND

Were I Less Fragile,

OUR FEET

I Would Be a Skateboarder!

Roger Connah

Where are we? We might be in a desert, sand blown by wind, shaped into known and unknown geometries. We might be in that inverted forest, a riposte to T. S. Eliot's *Waste Land*. The eye can pause in one of those concave refuges that wind offers, the desert we rarely experience. Or then we drift, a welcome illusion where the crest of a small mount is lopped off and the ground beneath our feet senses undulations of the tide. We register the perfect slice, a novel tectonic and precise cut, made by the contoured lines and forces that tempt no hierarchy. A beauty like sand dunes can still that moment for as long as we like. Mechanical and geometric precision coming from the most unusual sources – broken glass or the timeless waves – suggest not the banality of mini golf but urban mountaineering in strenuous miniature. Only much gentler.

It is quite possible we write about a piece of land, a plot, an urban square (which is never quite a square), a plaza, a piazza or a Platz, in ways that test our intuition. We sense the consistency of material and energy, these slow combustions that make up fresh expressions. We call it an interface and we still naturally think to other writing, though for how long we do not know, so rapidly does writing dissolve today. We see other diagrams of someone else's mind, even the "novel tectonics" of Reiser and Umemoto. And all this can remain so cruelly unreadable until we find a place that begins to make sense, that we imagine belongs to us, all of us. These tectonics, always a part of architecture's authentic jargon that we fall back on, make up the matter and energy that leads from, and makes up, actions which need no further communication. We feel, sense and register! This is a material practice which, according to Reiser and Umemoto, is "the shift from asking, what does this mean? to what does this do?"

Where should we start? Sitting, walking, smoking, vaping; ambling with less intent, or moving with more intent, a firm haste? Or skateboarding? This surface under our feet undulates ever so slightly, slopes indiscernibly around the large columned monument to those killed saving Austria. In this Platz-with-memory, Austria seems both under-feet in the earth, in the inverted forest and above, where the eagle is framed by mountain and sky. This makes for convincing but possibly redundant photography. The image less militant until, that is, we understand the shifts in time and history such monuments have gone through.

If I lived in Innsbruck, I would probably use this space regularly. If I had less fragility, I would learn to skateboard. Who dares, designs! Any part of this landscape may take eye and body into involuntary stillness. The space around us, surrounded by a diagram of rock, surprises. Is this a Noguchi in the city, and a de Chirico in the later afternoon shadows? Or is it seasalt with an aperitif? Reminding us how much diagrams always need that exit, in the afternoon past three o'clock the kids were out. A pair navigating the small inclines, kickflipping imaginary miniature rip curls in the textured concrete. Time and again the feet stall and the board is let go, running down on its own. When successful, the jubilant skateboarders perch with their boards stretched along the upper edge of the concrete. There must be a term or special code for this position. They hold their achievement. Queens and kings of their small smooth castle, astride, momentary statues. Then down.

We might also be in search of a coffee, an aperitif or digestif. We think to the spritz of dubious providence. Some will sit in the edge café with or without memory watching small children do what they do, run almost naked and take the water in the jets near the Landhaus. Unperturbed by eagle and monument, no screams just pure delight, kids called Wolf, Reiner, Suzi or Bennie. Shaded by four in the afternoon, the sun continues a shadow play through trees, whilst the re-skinned large black glass building frames, reflects and delicately distorts lines of mountain and eagle. After five or six o'clock the serious skaters, mountain bikers arrive, the BMXers; it is their playground. A persistent and consistent playground, not like a blank slate but as far away from those playground structures of controlled urban planning.

Some city spaces can accelerate, inviting public exit immediately on arrival. The exit is espied and destination practical and punctual. Others might be taking a pause from moving from one side of the "Platz" to the other, going from or towards the old town in Innsbruck. Other city spaces hold us back, ask for the idle moment, invite a turn, a pause. This is the wait where waiting is not always planned. This is the idling that allows us to breathe. In all cities, these urban moments are public invitations. They are channelled, directed through to the feet. For the feet recognise the pause. The "Platz" needs no memory then, it becomes the immediate. A clearing of space, light slanted through a dense forest. Just as a shadow bends to marry a deformed contour.

When is terra firma? When is the ground "grounded"? A terra firma forest is moist, tropical, one open to the seasonal flood that now encroaches. Terra firma also describes the mainland territories of the Republic of Venice. But terra firma is a rock group, a farscape and nearscape; a private equity firm and countless landscape companies. Disambiguation is something we must take seriously, and not because Wikipedia tells us so. Versatile and contextual we wish also for our mediations on the earth to be represented in other ways. Is not all that we consider a landscape, complex and dynamic, an unrevealed geometry waiting for novelty? And if so, do we seek the relational rules that guide – that ground us – realising the word ground is our very flexibility and existence. Terra Firma is also a brand of skateboard!

Terraforming, a term creeping into selected vocabularies in architecture and probably just as likely to disappear, has long been misunderstood. Coined by Jack Williamson in *Collision Orbit* (1942), it is this gentle science we see acted out in Innsbruck. Known as "earth-shaping" it is probably one of those actions we wish to have more than hypothetical content. Instead of deliberately modifying the atmosphere, temperature, surface topography or ecology of a planet, moon, or any other body that milks our energy, we consider smaller environments and wish to make them more habitable to dwell in. Every building alters the atmosphere, and not always to the good. Every landform can relieve it or ignore it. Architecture may have to become less about building and more about altering atmospheres. The deliberate modification of the contours of this city site invites new atmospheres; a small ecology of the horizon acting out in wind, climate and surface to become another anatomy. Accessibility and the layout of paths – machine patterns – result from the modulation of the surface. Spatial constraints, functional requirements offer a modelling glee and morphological precision. Becoming an imaginary space beyond its function, we still speak of urban planning for some reason.

A competition for a Students Union sited in the forest outside Helsinki was held in 1961. The land was solid, the outcrop exaggerated with firm geological layers that went down, down to that inverted forest. The tall trees were hardly a clearing but if you were reading Heidegger at the time, they could represent one. A young architect walked the site. Movements up and movements down suggested form and a diagram as rock began to function as roof and form. There was no trick about it. Successful action meant not to be seduced by the shadows and the light emerging through the trees. The architect would always say later he used his feet as sensors to measure the ground beneath, the slight incline, drag, concavity and depression. Changes were acute and subtle, geometry becoming space. A series of interlinked inverted caves became the well-known building Dipoli. Tempting myth to emerge, this was not merely a touching and misunderstood phenomenology, it was "morphology" where a precise geometry transformed an existing environment into a "constructed landscape". "The era in which we live," Kwinter writes in *The Judo of Cold Compulsion*, "can be characterised as one in which knowledge is increasingly devised from the structure of flow … (a) new materialism may well be a new expressionism." Contours and rates of change in data, patterns of material action. It was this new expressionism that emerged six decades ago to the young architect, Rema Pietilä.

We can speak of a terrain, a morphological act when form and structure of surface become part of the architectural eye. The ground beneath our feet became this Innsbruck project. Using digital modelling, always firing up the diagram in a private language until it gave precision, offered the architects those design exits required to become space. One can see an imagined roofscape, an earth that needs shaped uplift and depression. These were wired frames of site and space, new contours precisely planned, seen acutely on an aerial photograph. The cut, the contour, the shaping is applied by external and internal sensory morphology. We can speak now differently of topography and landforms. We can see the architect and the skateboarder kickflipping the diagram to make explosive geometry. Not in an art biennale, but here off grid and off the street.

The bright surface functions as a three-dimensional projection field. Protagonists together with the trees produce those high-contrast dynamics. The play of light and shade turning into night-time mountain shadow. What language helps us understand the precision and cold beauty of this work? Known by skateboarders as "Landi", the place holds immediate value and challenge. A suggested new way of reading this landform would be to use the words *convergence* and *divergence*. This is a model of cognition where tight spots emerge on the contour to be relieved, dispersed by more detached points. Spot-point-field; whatever vocabulary we resort to, we see the morphology, the topography and the terraforming all drawing out the intricacies of path and anti-path. Pedestrians and users, all protagonists in this theatre become observed and observing.

Not to skateboarders do we speak of tectonic lines, shifts in contour and content. Yet to the skateboarders this space too is "writing", a scripting using the body on the body of the work. Moving from supermarket car parks until moved on by the police, "Landi" is now freespace, a skaters' paradise. Wicked athletes they see themselves, they use the abbreviation "fav" for the word favourite, they live their own language as action, both creative scripting and challenging movement. "Landi" is a go-to place. Now many are sponsored, kickflipping their way through a photo-shoot at sunset. Insane plaza is the new street name for the challenges offered, jumping the landscape with its deceptively flat ground beneath their feet and board. Navigating those smooth curbs. Insane!

Do we see it through the software that has made the geometrical configurations possible? The surface texture of the concrete varies according to the type of geometrical configuration. Open joints, individual fields – this is the language of the architect and designer. Infrastructural elements shape the events which can take place anywhere on the square. All integrated in the construction and modulation of slab-fields of 100 m² (max) of in-situ concrete, joined by bolts that deal with shearing forces. No drainage pits visible on the site, drainage of the whole square including the fountains is located at the open joints between the individual fields. In one corner water is levelled into the stepped layers of the water sculpture. A new fractal perhaps, the designers create an innovative buffer system which, despite the existence of a subterranean garage, maintains all the visible surface water as it drains away within the landform. That is a neat trick.

This is "novel tectonics" akin to dress patterning. A manikin drawn horizontally, details pulled up, by the surgeon, the masseur, the forensic pathologist. The body takes shape. Material materialising in practice, matter and energy shaping the undulations, a layer of glass gravel holds the finishing top layer. A work meshed and sculptured on site, in the site, with the hand that strokes concrete until it held its density to form. This is a digital plasticity, where strokes are also human and field points on the site identified by slightly re-shifting the existing monuments on site. This is a post-mortem of land itself, a nip and tuck here or there where the redistribution of matter and energy, parts or details, become a surface within an organism. In careful, geometric relations cut by line and stencil, smoothed by digital meshing, informed by existing relations in a centre of the city, and formed and re-formed into what we could call a critical landscape. We get the sensory uplift of a reconstructed landscape.

In a city of spectres, marks and traces, Innsbruck becomes the careful arrangement of monument and memory. The atmosphere may be dominated by the rather leering facade of the Tyrolean provincial governmental building from the period of National Socialism facing the columned eagle-perching memorial. In spite of its visual appearance, the latter is a freedom monument commemorating the resistance against, and the liberation from, National Socialism. It acts as a giant cheese grater on site. Unequal memories unequally held are both rebellious and tranquil, this is less and less a "holy" backdrop. The memorial on its upset ground turns it into sorcery; an urban condition delightfully contradictory, unresolved and prone to delicious ambiguity. Here the architects have inserted a flat, water-spouting area between the Landhaus and the memorial. Artificial physical features of a blind spot; wet and dry where the presence of water, skateboarder and skinny dipper play against the monument's historical significance. This is not a scarred memory, but a necessarily blurred one. Just as low clouds slice off the top of the mountain that overlooks, overbears, overwhelms. This is a ghost form not so much ignoring any momentary new "reading" of history but seeking new relational depth.

"Did sea define the land or land the sea?" the Irish poet Seamus Heaney writes. We ask not quite the same for this landlocked gem, but we know how each part of the day and night draws new meaning from the collisions brought to Landhausplatz. It is not the sea which breaks on land to full identity, it is matter and action; the geometry of expressive disorder. We will end with a small passage from the *Atlas of Novel Tectonics*. We might have used several. The one finally chosen is not the only one relevant, but it offers "clues" to this critically welcoming space where others offer unfinished probes: "We hold to the idea that architecture is not simply reducible to the container and the contained but that there exists a dynamic exchange between the life of matter and the matter of our lives."

Wo befinden wir uns wohl? Möglicherweise in einer Wüste, der Wind spielt mit dem Sand, formt bekannte und unbekannte Geometrien. Vielleicht sind wir auch in jenem verkehrten Wald, einem Gegenentwurf zu T. S. Eliots *Waste Land*. Das Auge kann sich ausruhen an einem jener konkav-geformten Zufluchtsorte, die der Wind bereitstellt, die Wüste, die wir so wohl selten erleben. Oder wir lassen uns treiben, eine willkommene Illusion, bei welcher der Kamm eines kleinen Berges abgeschrägt ist und der Boden unter unseren Füßen die Wellenbewegungen der Gezeiten verspürt. Wir erkennen die perfekte Scheibe, einen neuartigen tektonischen Schnitt, verursacht durch die konturierten Linien und Kräfte, die sich jeglicher Hierarchie verschließen. Eine Schönheit wie eine Düne kann jenen Moment, solange wir wollen, festhalten. Mechanische und geometrische Präzision, die von den ungewöhnlichsten Quellen herrührt – zerbrochenem Glas oder zeitlosen Wellen –, erinnert nicht an die Banalität von Minigolf, sondern an urbanes Bergsteigen in kraftvollem Kleinformat. Nur viel sanfter.

Möglicherweise schreiben wir auch über ein Stück Land, eine Parzelle, einen städtischen Platz (der ja nie wirklich viereckig ist), eine Plaza, eine Piazza oder einen „Platz", und zwar auf eine Art und Weise, die unsere Intuition auf die Probe stellt. Wir fühlen die Beschaffenheit von Material und Energie, dieses langsame Abbrennen, welches neue, unverbrauchte Ausdrucksformen erschafft. Wir bezeichnen es als Schnittstelle und denken dabei natürlich an andere Schriften, obwohl wir nicht wissen, wie lange noch, so rasch löst sich das Geschriebene heutzutage auf. Wir sehen weitere Diagramme, entstanden in anderen Köpfen, sogar die „novel tectonics" von Reiser und Umemoto. Und all das kann auf so grausame Art unverständlich bleiben, bis wir einen Ort finden, der langsam einen Sinn ergibt, der in unserer Vorstellung uns gehört, uns allen. Diese Tektonik, immer ein Teil der authentischen Ausdrucksweise der Architektur, auf die wir zurückgreifen, bildet die Materie und Energie, die von Handlungen herrühren und sie erzeugen, welche keine weitere Kommunikation benötigen. Wir fühlen, spüren und halten fest! Es ist dies eine materielle Vorgehensweise, die nach Reiser und Umemoto „die Fragestellung von *was bedeutet das?* zu *was bewirkt das?* verändert."

Wo sollen wir beginnen? Beim Sitzen, Gehen, Rauchen, E-Zigaretten-Dampfen; beim Herumspazieren ohne Ziel oder bei einer zielgerichteten Bewegung, einer beständigen Eile? Oder beim Skateboard fahren? Diese Oberfläche unter unseren Füßen bewegt sich ganz leicht hin und her, steigt kaum wahrnehmbar um das große Säulendenkmal für die für Österreich Gefallenen an. Auf diesem Platz mit Vergangenheit erscheint Österreich sowohl unter den Füßen in der Erde, im verkehrten Wald und über uns, wo der Adler von Berg und Himmel eingerahmt wird. Das führt zu einer überzeugenden, aber möglicherweise überflüssigen Aufnahme. Das Bild erscheint uns weniger kämpferisch, wenn wir erst die zeitlichen und geschichtlichen Veränderungen verstehen, die solch Denkmäler durchlaufen haben.

Lebte ich in Innsbruck, würde ich diesen Platz wahrscheinlich regelmäßig benutzen. Wenn ich weniger zerbrechlich wäre, würde ich lernen Skateboard zu fahren. Wer wagt, entwirft! Jeder Teil dieser Landschaft kann Auge und Körper in unfreiwillige Stille versetzen. Der Raum um uns, umgeben von einem steinigen Diagramm aus Felsen, überrascht. Ist das ein Noguchi in der Stadt und ein de Chirico im Schatten des späteren Nachmittags? Oder ist es Meersalz mit einem Aperitif? Wie sehr Diagramme immer solch einen Ausgang brauchen, wird uns bewusst am Nachmittag nach drei Uhr, wenn die Kids auf dem Platz sind. Ein Paar navigiert an den kleinen Steigungen entlang, macht Kickflips über winzige imaginäre Wölbungen im strukturierten Beton. Immer wieder bleiben die Füße stehen und geben das Board frei, das von allein nach unten rollt. Wenn es gelingt, dann balancieren die jubelnden Skateboarder*innen mit ihren in die Luft ragenden Boards entlang des oberen Betonrandes. Für diese Position muss es sicherlich einen Ausdruck oder Spezialbegriff geben. Sie halten ihre Leistung fest. Königinnen und Könige ihres kleinen glatten Schlosses, wie Reiter*innen, kurzzeitige Statuen. Dann wieder hinunter.

Vielleicht befinden wir uns auch auf der Suche nach einer Tasse Kaffee, einem Aperitif oder Digestif. Wir denken an den Gespritzten mit zweifelhafter Abstammung? Einige sitzen wohl im Café am Rande des Platzes und erinnern sich, oder auch nicht, daran, was kleine Kinder so machen, halbnackt herumlaufen und mit dem Wasser des Sprühbrunnens nahe dem Landhaus spielen. Unbeeindruckt von Adler und Denkmal, kein Geschrei, nur reine Freude, Kinder, die Wolf, Reiner, Suzi oder Bennie heißen. Im Vier-Uhr-Nachmittags-Schatten setzt die Sonne ihr Schattenspiel durch die Bäume fort, während das neu verkleidete große schwarze Gebäude die Konturen des Berges und des Adlers einrahmt, widerspiegelt und grazil verzerrt. Nach fünf oder sechs Uhr treffen die professionellen Skater*innen, Mountainbiker*innen, die BMXler*innen ein, schließlich ist es ihr Spielplatz. Ein beständiger und verlässlicher Spielplatz, nicht wie eine unbeschriebene Tafel, sondern meilenweit entfernt von all jenen klar strukturierten Spielplätzen der kontrollierten Stadtplanung.

Manche Stadtplätze haben beschleunigende Wirkung, fordern die Öffentlichkeit schon bei der Ankunft zum Verlassen auf. Man erspäht den Ausgang und erreicht das Ziel auf praktische und pünktliche Art. Andere machen vielleicht eine Pause, während sie sich von der einen Platzhälfte zur anderen bewegen und dabei entweder von der Innsbrucker Altstadt kommen oder sich auf sie zu bewegen. Andere Plätze in der Stadt halten uns zurück, laden uns zum Nichtstun, zum Umkehren, zu einer Pause ein. Das ist die Wartezeit, die nicht wirklich eingeplant ist. Das ist der Leerlauf, der uns zu Atem kommen lässt. In allen Städten sind diese urbanen Augenblicke wie eine öffentliche Einladung. Sie werden kanalisiert und bis zu den Füßen weitergeleitet. Denn die Füße erkennen die Pause genau. Der Platz braucht dann nicht wirklich ein Gedächtnis, er wird zum Unmittelbaren. Eine Lichtung im Raum, Licht, das schräg durch einen dichten Wald einfällt. So wie sich ein Schatten neigt, um sich mit einer deformierten Kontur zu vermählen.

Wann ist Terra *firma* – also *fest*? Wann ist der Boden geerdet? Ein Terra-firma-Wald ist feucht, tropisch, anfällig für saisonale Überschwemmungen, die nun auftreten. Terra firma beschreibt auch die Gebiete der Republik Venedig auf dem Festland. Aber Terra firma ist eine Felsengruppe, eine weit entfernte und nahe Landschaft; eine private Kapitalgesellschaft und zahlreiche Landschaftsfirmen. Begriffserklärungen sollten wir ernst nehmen, und nicht nur, weil Wikipedia uns dazu rät. Vielseitig und kontextabhängig wünschen wir, dass unsere Mediationen auf der Erde auch auf andere Art dargestellt werden. Ist nicht alles, das wir als Landschaft ansehen, komplex und dynamisch, eine unentdeckte Geometrie, die auf den Reiz des Neuen wartet? Und wenn ja, suchen wir dann die Beziehungsregeln, die uns führen und erden im Bewusstsein, dass der Begriff „erden“ unsere Flexibilität und Existenz ausmacht? Terra Firma ist übrigens auch eine Skateboard-Marke!

Terraforming, ein Ausdruck, der sich langsam in das ausgewählte Vokabular der Architektur eingeschlichen hat und wahrscheinlich ebenso rasch wieder verschwinden wird, ist lange Zeit missverstanden worden. Erstmals verwendet von Jack Williamson in *Collision Orbit* (1942), beschreibt er diese sanfte Wissenschaft, die wir in Innsbruck vorgeführt bekommen. Auch bekannt als *earth-shaping* (Erde gestaltend) ist sie wahrscheinlich eine jener

Aktionen, die wir einem hypothetischen Inhalt vorziehen würden. Statt bewusst die Atmosphäre, Temperatur, Flächentopografie oder Ökologie eines Planeten, Mondes oder anderen Körpers, der uns Energie kostet, zu verändern, betrachten wir kleinere Umgebungen und wünschen uns, wir könnten sie bewohnbarer machen, um dort zu leben. Jedes Gebäude verändert die Atmosphäre, und nicht immer zum Guten. Jede Landschaftsform kann sie entlasten oder ignorieren. Vielleicht sollte Architektur weniger mit dem Bauen zu tun haben als vielmehr mit dem Verändern der Atmosphären. Die bewusste Modifikation der Konturen dieses städtischen Ortes fordert zu neuen Atmosphären heraus; eine kleine Ökologie des Horizontes, ausgelebt im Wind, Klima und der Oberfläche, um sich in eine andere Anatomie zu verwandeln. Die Zugänglichkeit und die Gestaltung der Wege – Maschinenmuster – ergeben sich aus der Anpassung der Oberfläche. Räumliche Einschränkungen, funktionale Anforderungen bieten Gestaltungsfreude und morphologische Präzision. Wenn ein imaginärer Raum jenseits seiner Funktion entsteht, dann sprechen wir dennoch aus gutem Grund von Stadtplanung.

Im Jahre 1961 wurde ein Wettbewerb für ein Gebäude der Studierendenvertretung in einem Wald außerhalb von Helsinki ausgeschrieben. Der Boden war solide, der Aufschluss überhöht mit festen geologischen Schichten, die tief in jenen verkehrten Wald hinunterreichten. Die hohen Bäume bildeten nicht wirklich eine Lichtung, aber wenn man zu jener Zeit Heidegger las, dann könnte man sich schon eine Lichtung vorstellen. Der junge Architekt schritt den Bauplatz ab. Die Auf- und Abbewegungen suggerierten eine Form und ein Diagramm. Der Fels begann, als Dach und Form zu wirken. Dabei gab es keinen Trick. Erfolgreiches Handeln bedeutete, sich nicht von den Schatten und dem Licht, das durch die Bäume drang, verführen zu lassen. Später würde der Architekt immer wieder behaupten, er hätte seine Füße als Sensoren verwendet, um den Boden unter ihm zu vermessen, die leichte Neigung, Umtiefung, Wölbung und Senkung zu vermessen. Die Veränderungen waren zugleich intensiv und subtil, Geometrie, die sich in Raum verwandelte. Eine Reihe von miteinander verbundenen umgekehrten Höhlen wurde zu dem bekannten Gebäude Dipoli. Versucht, einen Mythos zu erschaffen, war das nicht nur eine berührende und falsch verstandene Phänomenologie, sondern es war eine Morphologie, bei der eine genaue Geometrie eine real existierende Umgebung in eine „konstruierte Landschaft" verwandelte. „Das Zeitalter, in dem wir leben, kann beschrieben werden als eines, bei dem Wissen sich in zunehmendem Maße von der Struktur des Fließens entwickelt", schreibt Kwinter in *The Judo of Cold Compulsion* (*Das Judo des kalten Zwanges*), „der neue Materialismus ist vielleicht ein neuer Expressionismus." Konturen und Veränderungsgrade bei Daten, Mustern und materiellen Handlungen; es war dieser neue Expressionismus, der sich vor sechs Jahrzehnten bei dem jungen Architekten Rema Pietilä herausbildete.

Wir können von einem Terrain oder Gelände sprechen, einem morphologischen Akt, wenn Form und Struktur der Oberfläche Teil des architektonischen Blickes werden. *Der Boden unter unseren Füßen* wurde dieses Projekt in Innsbruck. Der Einsatz von digitaler Modellierung, die das Diagramm so lange in eine private Sprache übersetzte, bis Präzision eintrat, bot den Architekt*innen jene Entwurfsausgänge, die notwendig sind, um zu Raum zu werden. Man erblickt eine imaginäre Dachlandschaft, eine Erde, die geformte Hebungen und Senkungen benötigt. Diese waren verdrahtete Rahmen von Standort und Raum, neue, präzise geplante Konturen, auf einer Luftaufnahme genau erkennbar. Der Schnitt, die Kontur, die Formgebung wird durch externe und interne sensorische Morphologie ausgeführt. Wir können in diesem Zusammenhang anders von Topografie und Landschaftsform sprechen. Wir können Architekt*innen und Skateboarder*innen sehen, wie sie im Diagramm kickflippen, um explosive Geometrie zu erzeugen. Nicht im Rahmen einer Kunstbiennale, sondern in diesem Fall jenseits des Rasters und abseits der Straße.

Die helle Oberfläche fungiert als dreidimensionales Projektionsfeld. Gemeinsam mit den Bäumen erzeugen die Protagonist*innen diese kontrastreiche Dynamik. Das Spiel von Licht und Schatten wird zum nächtlichen Bergschatten. Welche Sprache hilft uns dabei, die Präzision und kalte Schönheit dieser Arbeit zu verstehen? Der von den Skateboarder*innen als „Landi" bezeichnete Platz besitzt direkten Nutzen und ist eine Herausforderung. Ein Vorschlag für eine neue Art, diese Landschaftsform zu lesen, wäre die Verwendung der Begriffe *Konvergenz* und *Divergenz*. Das ist ein Modell der Wahrnehmung, bei dem straffe Punkte auf der Kontur auftauchen, um sich dann durch weiter entfernte Punkte zu lösen und zu zerstreuen. Fleck-Punkt-Feld – welch Begriffe wir auch verwenden mögen, so sehen wir, wie die Morphologie, die Topografie und das *Terraforming* gemeinsam die Feinheiten von Weg und Anti-Weg aufzeigen. Fußgänger*innen und Benutzer*innen, alle Protagonist*innen dieses Theaters werden beobachtet und beobachten.

Nicht mit den Skateboarder*innen wollen wir über tektonische Linien, Verschiebungen in der Kontur und im Inhalt sprechen. Doch gerade für die Skateboarder*innen ist dieser Raum auch etwas „Geschriebenes", ein Schreiben des Körpers auf dem Körper des Werkes. Der Weg führte vom Skateboarden auf Supermarktparkplätzen, bis die Polizei sie vertrieb, hin zum „Landi", dem neuen *Freespace* (Freiraum), einem Paradies für Skater*innen. Als böse Athlet*innen sehen sie sich selbst, verwenden die Abkürzung „fav" für das Wort *favourite* (Lieblings-), sie leben ihre eigene Sprache als Aktion aus, sowohl kreatives Schreiben also auch faszinierende Bewegung. Der „Landi" ist ein beliebter Treffpunkt. Inzwischen werden viele gesponsert, wenn sie sich bei Sonnenuntergang mit Kickflips durch ein Fotoshooting bewegen. *Insane plaza* (verrückter Platz) ist der neue Straßenname für die Herausforderungen, die sich ihnen bieten, wenn sie über die Landschaft mit ihrem trügerisch flachen Boden unter ihren Füßen und Boards springen. An jenen abgerundeten Bordkanten entlang – einfach wahnsinnig!

Sehen wir es vielleicht durch die Software, die diese geometrischen Strukturen erst möglich gemacht hat? Die Oberflächenbeschaffenheit des Betons variiert entsprechend der Art der geometrischen Figur. Offene Verbindungsstellen, einzelne Felder – das ist die Sprache der Architekt*innen und der Designer*innen. Infrastrukturelle Elemente formen die Ereignisse, die sich überall auf dem Platz abspielen können. Alles ist integriert in die Konstruktion und Modulation von Plattenfeldern aus maximal 100 Quadratmeter Ortbeton, verbunden durch Bolzen, welche die Scherkräfte ableiten. Auf dem Platz sind keine Entwässerungsgruben sichtbar, die Entwässerung des ganzen Platzes inklusive des Brunnens erfolgt durch die offenen Verbindungen zwischen den einzelnen Feldern. In einer Ecke wird das Wasser über die abgestuften Schichten der Wasserskulptur abgeleitet. Vielleicht ein neues Fraktal, denn die Designer*innen schaffen ein neuartiges Puffersystem, das trotz der darunterliegenden Tiefgarage das gesamte sichtbare Oberflächenwasser auffängt, obwohl es innerhalb der Geländeform versickert. Das ist ein raffinierter Trick.

Hier handelt es sich um „neue Tektonik", ähnlich den Mustern von Kleidern. Ein Körper, waagerecht gezeichnet, der von Chirurg*innen, Masseur*innen und Gerichtsmediziner*innen mit Details versehen wurde. Der Körper nimmt Gestalt an. Material, das sich in der Ausführung materialisiert, Materie und Energie formen die Wellen, eine Schicht aus Glaskieseln hält die abschließende oberste Schicht zusammen. Ein Werk, das vor Ort ineinandergreift und Form annimmt, im Ort selbst, durch die Hand, die den Beton streichelt, bis er seine Dichte in eine Form verwandelt. Es ist dies eine digitale Plastizität, bei der auch die Striche menschlich sind und Feldpunkte auf dem Platz durch das leichte Verschieben von bestehenden lokalen Denkmälern festgelegt werden.
Es ist ein Post-Mortem des Geländes selbst, ein Hin- und Herziehen da und dort, wo die Neuverteilung von Materie und Energie, von Teilen und Details innerhalb eines Organismus zu einer Oberfläche verschmilzt. In sorgfältigen, geometrischen Relationen, durch Linien und Schablonen geschnitten, geglättet durch digitale Vermaschung, durch bestehende Relationen in einem Stadtzentrum inspiriert, und geformt und umgeformt zu dem, was wir als eine kritische Landschaft bezeichnen könnten. Wir erhalten die sinnliche Steigerung einer rekonstruierten Landschaft.

In einer Stadt aus Schemen, Zeichen und Spuren entwickelt sich Innsbruck zu einer sorgfältigen Anordnung von Denkmal und Erinnerung. Die Atmosphäre mag wohl beherrscht werden von der starrenden Fassade des Gebäudes der Tiroler Landesregierung, das aus der Zeit des Nationalsozialismus stammt und dem Kriegsdenkmal mit den Säulen und dem aufgesetzten Adler gegenüberliegt. Trotz seines Erscheinungsbildes ist Letzteres ein Freiheitsdenkmal, das an den Widerstand gegen den und die Befreiung vom Nationalsozialismus erinnert. Es wirkt an diesem Ort wie eine riesige Käsereibe. Unterschiedliche Erinnerungen wirken auf unterschiedliche Weise nach und sind sowohl rebellisch als auch friedvoll, die Kulisse hier wird immer weniger „heilig". Das Denkmal auf gekipptem Boden verwandelt sie in Zauberei; ein urbaner Zustand, erfrischend widersprüchlich, ungelöst und anfällig für köstliche Zweideutigkeit. Hier haben die Architekt*innen eine flache, wasserspeiende Zone zwischen Landhaus und Denkmal eingefügt. Künstlich entstandene Merkmale im toten Winkel; nass und trocken, dort wo Wasser, Skateboarder*innen und Badende gegen die historische Bedeutung des Denkmals auf-/antreten. Das ist keine Erinnerung mit Narben, sondern eine notwendigerweise verschwommene. Genauso wie tief hängende Wolken die Bergspitzen, die sie überragen, überwältigen und erdrücken, abschneiden. Es ist dies eine Geistergestalt, die nicht eine zeitgenössische „Lesart" von Geschichte ignoriert, sondern eine neue Beziehungstiefe sucht.

„Hat das Meer das Land oder das Land das Meer definiert?", schreibt der irische Dichter Seamus Heaney. Wir stellen uns zwar bei diesem Binnenkleinod nicht diese Frage, aber wir wissen, wie jede Tages- und Nachtzeit eine neue Bedeutung aus den Kollisionen auf der Landhaus-Plaza hervorbringt. Es ist nicht das Meer, das sich erst durch das Land definiert, es sind Materie und Handlung; die Geometrie einer expressiven Unordnung. Wir wollen mit einem kurzen Auszug aus dem *Atlas der neuen Tektonik* schließen. Da gäbe es freilich einige. Der letztlich ausgewählte ist nicht der einzig relevante, jedoch gibt er Hinweise auf diesen kritisch einladenden Raum, wo andere nur unvollständige Ansätze bieten: „Wir halten an der Vorstellung fest, dass Architektur nicht einfach auf den Behälter und das darin Enthaltene reduziert werden kann, sondern dass ein dynamischer Austausch existiert zwischen dem Leben der Materie und den Angelegenheiten unseres Lebens."

Roger Connah is an architect, architectural publicist, curator and filmmaker and has been teaching architecture and architectural theory at several universities for over three decades. In 2001 he founded the Heron-Mazy Studio with John Maruszczak and in 2008 he won the first prize at the White House Redux competition. Between 2009 and 2020 Connah was a professor at the Azrieli School of Architecture & Urbanism at Carleton University in Ottawa, Canada. He is currently Curator at the Canadian Center of Mindful Habitats in Ottawa and Professor at the Avani Institute in Koshikode, Kerala, India.

Throughout his career, Connah has specialised in the history of Finnish architecture. In addition, he has curated numerous exhibitions, made films and published books.

Roger Connah ist Architekt, Architekturpublizist, Kurator und Filmemacher und lehrt seit über drei Jahrzehnten Architektur und Architekturtheorie an verschiedenen Universitäten. Im Jahr 2001 gründete er mit John Maruszczak das Heron-Mazy Studio, 2008 gewann er den ersten Preis beim Wettbewerb White House Redux. Von 2009 bis 2020 war Connah Professor an der Azrieli School of Architecture & Urbanism der Carleton University in Ottawa, Kanada. Derzeit ist er Kurator am Canadian Center of Mindful Habitats in Ottawa und Professor am Avani Institute in Koshikode, Kerala, Indien.

Im Laufe seiner Karriere hat sich Connah auf die Geschichte der finnischen Architektur spezialisiert. Darüber hinaus hat er zahlreiche Ausstellungen kuratiert und Filme und Bücher veröffentlicht.

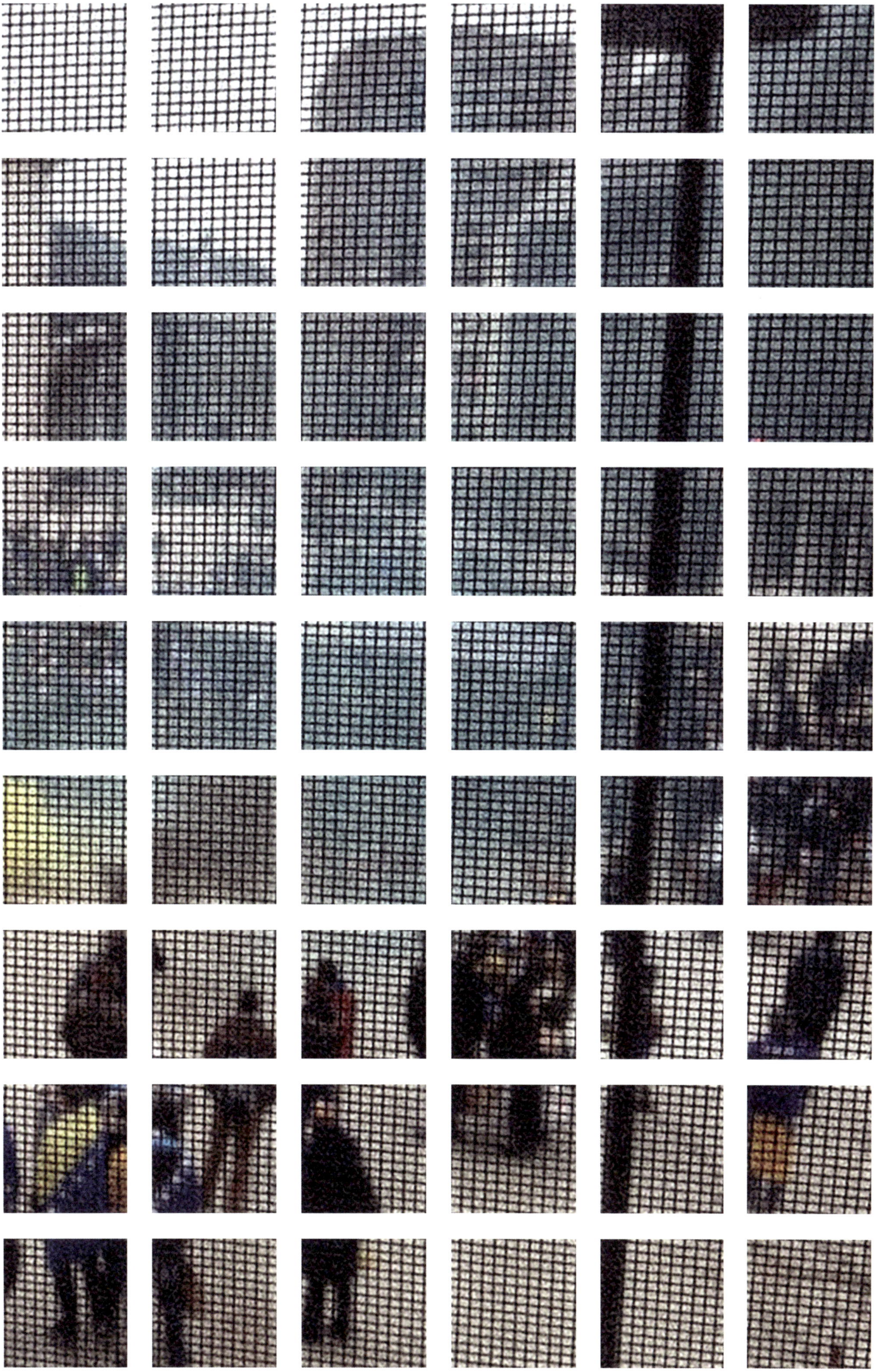

A FORM OF RESISTANCE

Florian Waldvogel

According to the novelist Marcel Proust, the true paradises are those that we have lost. But this is not the case in Innsbruck, where Landhausplatz can still be found right in the heart of the city. Where another city might have succumbed to financial interests, Innsbruck opted for a project that critically addresses and shapes the square in front of the district offices that was once the parade ground of the Nazis and of Tyrol's own Kaiserjäger regiments.

Hence, the immediate attraction of Landhausplatz is the fact that it is a stage that requires no dramatic words. It derives its strength from the recognition that it mediates in a different, more extravagant way: from the recognition of its own exclusion, its exclusion from the codified world of the design of public squares.

In its most intense moments, in its beauty, vulnerability and despair, Landhausplatz presents an unwavering and powerful image. The life of the square and its own performative appropriation of this life make us witnesses to the urban resistance triggered by the psyche of the place. The architects provocatively challenged its representative function with their design of physical and performative activities that counteract the classic functional and regulative constraints of public spaces. By creating new spatial and temporal patterns, they confront the regulating logic of profit, efficiency, control and normality. As a result, Landhausplatz questions the notions that urban space is only there to be obeyed and that our only role in such space is to act as efficient machines in the processes of exchange and accumulation. The design opens up a forum that heralds the transition from objects to activities, from design to creative experience. The project offers us a return to architecture as not only form but also temporal and spatial negotiation, as the interaction with objects that are unreservedly open to all, not as exclusive goods but as the shared good of social experience.

In their creative considerations, the design team examined the power structures of Landhausplatz as a means of criticising the associated nationalism, sexism and racism as well as the related capitalist production. They addressed the issue of memory by adopting a cultural grammar that reflects upon these power structures and establishes starting points for questioning them. The entire square is covered by an undulating concrete shell that rises and falls and, rather than hiding the history of the square, sheds light on those critical clues to this history that have been hidden by the Province of Tyrol as a means of polishing the image of the city and correcting its collective memory.

Landhausplatz and the tools of landscape design also offer an ideal setting for those strategies of subversion that, under the title "street skateboarding", are employed as ways of appropriating, transforming, parodying and even alienating architecture and urban design.

Much of urban architecture is destined for the production of things – things in the form of goods and immaterial work. In this sense, places such as buildings and squares play a part in this process of production. Skateboarding, on the other hand, makes no such contribution. It consumes a place without participating in its economic productivity, as a result of which it is a performative equivalent of architectural ideas.

In this way, Landhausplatz demonstrates the reinvigoration of the urban not as a product but as a way of life and confirms Henri Lefebvre's slogan from 1968 that "the beach lies beneath the paving stones".

Dem Romancier Marcel Proust zufolge sind die wahren Paradiese stets die, welche man verloren hat. Nicht so in Innsbruck: Dort gibt es mitten in der Stadt den Landhausplatz. Wo andere Städte monetären Interessen nachgeben, entschied man sich für ein Projekt, das sich einer kritischen Aufarbeitung und Gestaltung des ehemaligen Aufmarschplatzes der Nazis sowie der Tiroler Kaiserjäger vor dem Gau-Haus stellte.

Der Landhausplatz ist eine Bühne ohne große Worte, daher rührt seine unmittelbare Anziehungskraft. Die Stärke dieses Ortes liegt in der Erkenntnis, dass er anders ist in seiner extravaganten Mediation. Es ist dieses Erkennen der eigenen Ausgeschlossenheit, einer Ausgeschlossenheit aus der kodifizierten Welt der Platzgestaltung.

Der Landhausplatz ist in seinen intensivsten Momenten, seiner Schönheit, seiner Verletzlichkeit und seiner Verzweiflung ein ungebrochenes und machtvolles Bild. Durch das Leben selbst und seine performative Aneignung werden wir Zeug*innen des urbanen Widerstands, der über die Psyche des Ortes erfolgt. Die Architekt*innen konterten das Repräsentative und provozierten mit ihrer Gestaltung körperzentrierte und performative Aktivitäten, welche den funktionalen und regulativen Zwängen öffentlicher Räume entgegenwirken. Indem sie neue Raum- und Zeitmuster schaffen, kritisieren sie die regulierende Logik von Profit, Effizienz, Kontrolle und Normalität. Der Landhausplatz stellt daher die Vorstellung infrage, dass der städtische Raum allein dazu da ist, um ihm gehorsam Folge zu leisten; und dass wir nur als effiziente Automaten in den Prozessen des Tauschs und der Akkumulation existieren. Die Gestaltung eröffnet ein Forum, welches den Übergang von Dingen zu Werken, von Design zu kreativer Erfahrung andeutet. Das Projekt bietet eine Rückkehr zur Architektur nicht nur als Form, sondern als Verhandlung von Zeit und Raum, als Auseinandersetzung mit Objekten, die uneingeschränkt jeder und jedem zur Verfügung stehen – nicht als Ware, vielmehr als gemeinsames Gut sozialer Erfahrung.

Die gestalterischen Überlegungen des Entwurfsteams untersuchten die Herrschaftsverhältnisse des Landhausplatzes und kritisieren den damit verbundenen Nationalismus, Sexismus, Rassismus und die mit ihnen verknüpfte kapitalistische Produktion. Die Gestaltung der Erinnerungskultur betrachtet die Herrschaftsverhältnisse in den Formen der kulturellen Grammatik und formuliert Ansatz-punkte dafür, wie sie hinterfragt werden können. Der gesamte Platz wird von einem wellenförmigen, auf- und absteigenden Betonmantel geschützt, der nicht verdeckt, sondern präzise jene kritischen Hinweise zur Geschichte des Platzes offenbart, welche vom Land Tirol verdrängt, zugunsten der städtischen Imagepflege kaschiert und so im kollektiven Gedächtnis der Stadt nie da waren.

Die Landhausplatz- bzw. Landschaftsgestaltung bietet aber außerdem eine ideale Voraussetzung für jene Subversionsstrategien, die unter dem Begriff „Streetskaten" in Formen der Aneignung, der Transformation, der Parodie sowie der Verfremdung von Architektur und Urbanität zur Anwendung kommen.

Ein Großteil der urbanen Architektur ist für die Produktion von Dingen gedacht – Dingen in Form von Waren und immaterieller Arbeit. In diesem Sinne sind Gebäude, Plätze etc. Orte, die in die Produktion und Verteilung von Dingen eingebunden sind. Skateboarding hingegen leistet keinen solchen Beitrag, es konsumiert den Ort, ohne an seiner ökonomischen Produktivität teilzunehmen, und ist sonach eine performative Entsprechung der architektonischen Gedanken.

Der Landhausplatz verweist somit auf die Wiederbelebung des Urbanen nicht als ein Produkt, sondern als Lebensweise, und bestätigt den Slogan von Henri Lefebvre aus dem Jahr 1968, demzufolge „unter den Pflastersteinen der Strand liegt".

Florian Waldvogel is a curator and editor of numerous publications on contemporary art. He studied Praxis der Kunstvermittlung at the Academy of Fine Arts Städelschule in Frankfurt am Main. He was artistic director at Kokerei Zollverein | Contemporary Art and Criticism in Essen, co-curator of *Just Do It!* in Linz 2005, *Manifesta 6* in Nicosia, Cyprus 2006 and *A 37 90 89 – The Invention of the Neo-Avant-Garde* in Berlin 2018. From 2006 to 2008 he was curator at Witte de With in Rotterdam and from 2009 to 2013 director of the Kunstverein in Hamburg. Since June 2019, he has headed the Modern Collection at the Tyrolean State Museums in Innsbruck. Waldvogel is, among others, editor of *I Have Seen the Future* by Kiki Kogelnik (2012) as well as *Tom Kummer – Reportages and Portraits 1987-2016* (2020), co-editor of *Handbuch Antirassismus* (2002), *Critical Condition* by Julie Ault and Martin Beck (2003), *Freedom of Speech* (2011), *Oh Kunstverein, Where Art Thou?* (2013), *Handlung als Haltung – Zentrum für politische Schönheit* (2017) as well as *Atlas* by Gelatin/gelitin (2022). Author of *Who Let the Dogs Out* (2001), *Libretto for a Possible Kunstverein* (2010) and *Aspects of the Curatorial using Kasper König as an example* (2016).

Waldvogel also teaches at various universities.

Florian Waldvogel ist Ausstellungsmacher und Herausgeber zahlreicher Publikationen zur Gegenwartskunst. Er studierte Praxis der Kunstvermittlung an der Staatlichen Hochschule für Bildende Künste Städelschule in Frankfurt am Main. Er war künstlerischer Leiter an der Kokerei Zollverein | Zeitgenössische Kunst und Kritik in Essen, Co-Kurator von *Just Do It!* in Linz 2005, der *Manifesta 6* in Nicosia, Zypern, 2006 und *A 37 90 89 – Die Erfindung der Neo-Avantgarde* in Berlin 2018. Von 2006 bis 2008 war er Kurator am Witte de With in Rotterdam und von 2009 bis 2013 Direktor des Kunstvereins in Hamburg. Seit Juni 2019 ist er Leiter der Modernen Sammlung an den Tiroler Landesmuseen in Innsbruck. Waldvogel ist u.a. Herausgeber von *I Have Seen the Future* von Kiki Kogelnik (2012) sowie von *Tom Kummer – Reportagen und Porträts 1987-2016* (2020), Mitherausgeber von *Handbuch Antirassismus* (2002), *Critical Condition* von Julie Ault und Martin Beck (2003), *Freedom of Speech* (2011), *Oh Kunstverein, Where Art Thou?* (2013), *Handlung als Haltung – Zentrum für politische Schönheit* (2017) als auch *Atlas* von Gelatin/gelitin (2022). Er ist Autor von *Who Let the Dogs Out* (2001), *Libretto für einen möglichen Kunstverein* (2010) und *Aspekte des Kuratorischen am Beispiel Kasper König* (2016).

Zudem unterrichtet Waldvogel an diversen Universitäten.

IF I CAN'T DANCE, I DON'T WANNA BE PART OF YOUR REVOLUTION IF I CAN'T DANCE, I DON

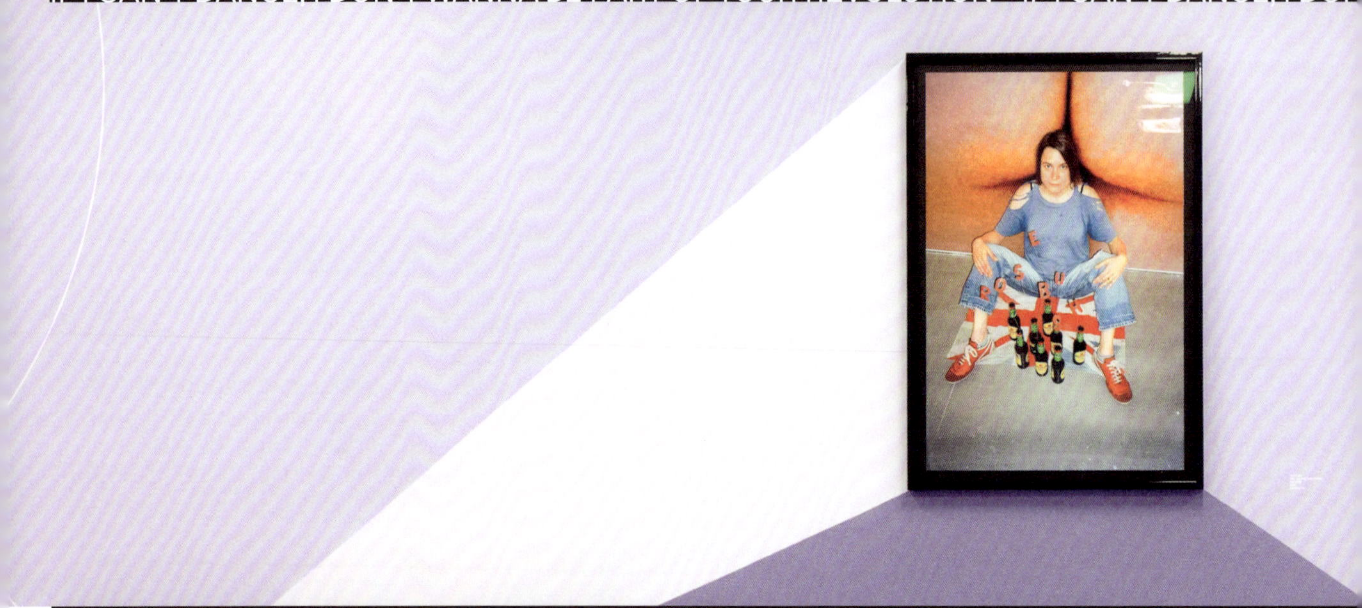

REVOLUTION IF I CAN'T DANCE, I DON'T WANNA BE PART OF YOUR REVOLUTION IF I CAN'

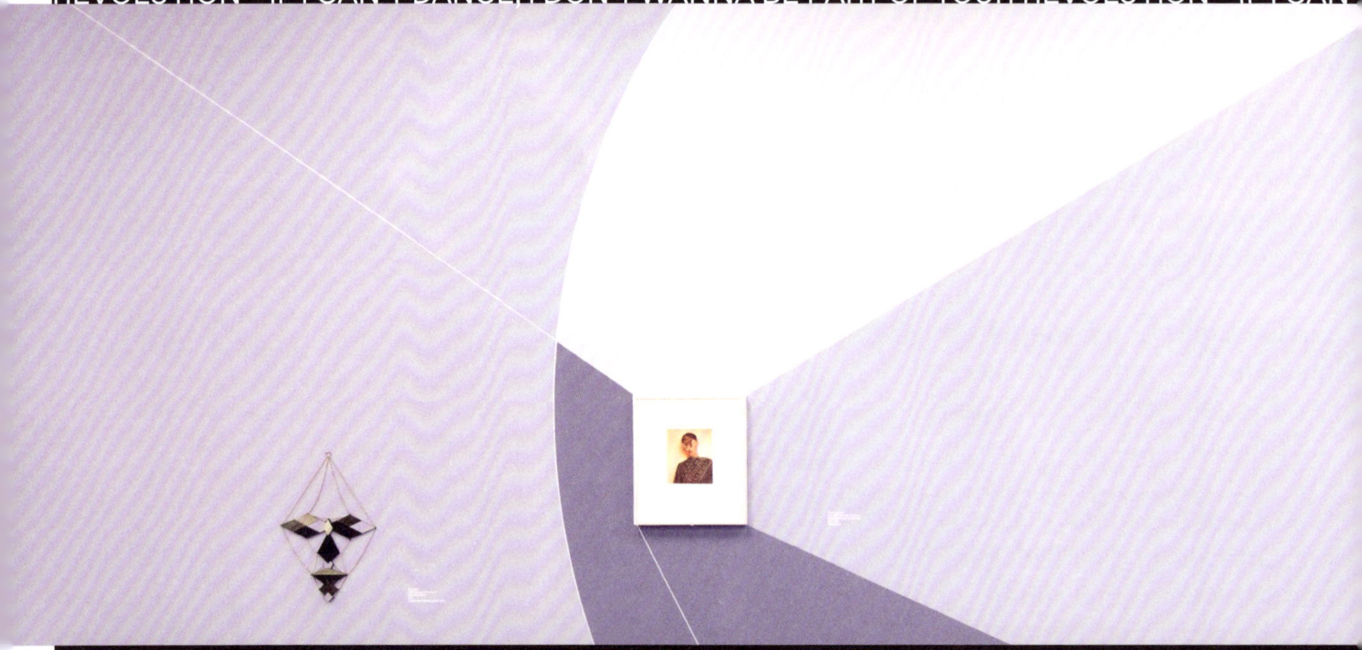

BE PART OF YOUR REVOLUTION IF I CAN'T DANCE, I DON'T WANNA BE PART OF YOUR REVO

I DON'T WANNA BE PART OF YOUR REVOLUTION IF I CAN'T DANCE, I DON'T WANNA BE PAR

A BE PART OF YOUR REVOLUTION IF I CAN'T DANCE, I DON'T WANNA BE PART OF YOUR

I DON'T WANNA BE PART OF YOUR REVOLUTION IF I CAN'T DANCE, I DON'T WANNA

IF I CAN'T DANCE, I DON'T WANNA BE PART OF YOUR REVOLUTION IF I CAN'T DANCE,

R REVOLUTION IF I CAN'T DANCE, I DON'T WANNA BE PART OF YOUR REVOLUTION

"IF I CAN'T DANCE, I DON'T WANNA BE PART OF YOUR REVOLUTION" (2020)
Feminist Positions from the Modern Collection of the Tiroler Landesmuseen / Ferdinandeum.

Curated by Florian Waldvogel

„IF I CAN'T DANCE, I DON'T WANNA BE PART OF YOUR REVOLUTION" (2020)
Feministische Positionen aus der Modernen Sammlung der Tiroler Landesmuseen / Ferdinandeum.

Kuratiert von Florian Waldvogel

ischia

PMA	P2 Urban Hybrid	2018	Residential building Public space	Innsbruck Austria
PROJECT	TITLE	YEAR	SUBJECT	LOCATION

Ideally, architectural concepts should be able to shape public and private relationships and interests in such a way that an innovative topos is created which is able to promote both the day-to-day and the cultural lives of a city. P2 performs this challenging balancing act by bringing together a range of functions in an architecturally differentiated and yet spatially limited volume that consists of a base, a square and a tower. The spatial interaction between the individual volumes follows a logic that is both internally compositional and externally urban.

Hence, as soon as the investor and the municipality complete their deal, the dynamic multifunctional use of the object will be able to follow.

Im besten Fall sind architektonische Konzepte in der Lage, öffentliche und private Beziehungen und Interessen so zu gestalten, dass dabei ein innovativer Topos entsteht, der Stadtleben und -kultur fördert. Das P2 macht diesen herausfordernden Spagat, indem es unterschiedliche Funktionen in einem architektonisch differenzierten und dennoch räumlich verschränkten Baukörper, bestehend aus Sockel, Platz und Turm, vereint. Das räumliche Zusammenspiel der einzelnen Volumen folgt dabei sowohl einer kompositorisch inneren als auch einer stadträumlichen äußeren Logik.

Eine multifunktionale lebendige Nutzung könnte folgen, würden der Investor und die Stadt ihren Deal endlich vollziehen.

PEMA 2

Kulturplateau layout, second floor

Grundriss Kulturplateau 2. Obergeschoss

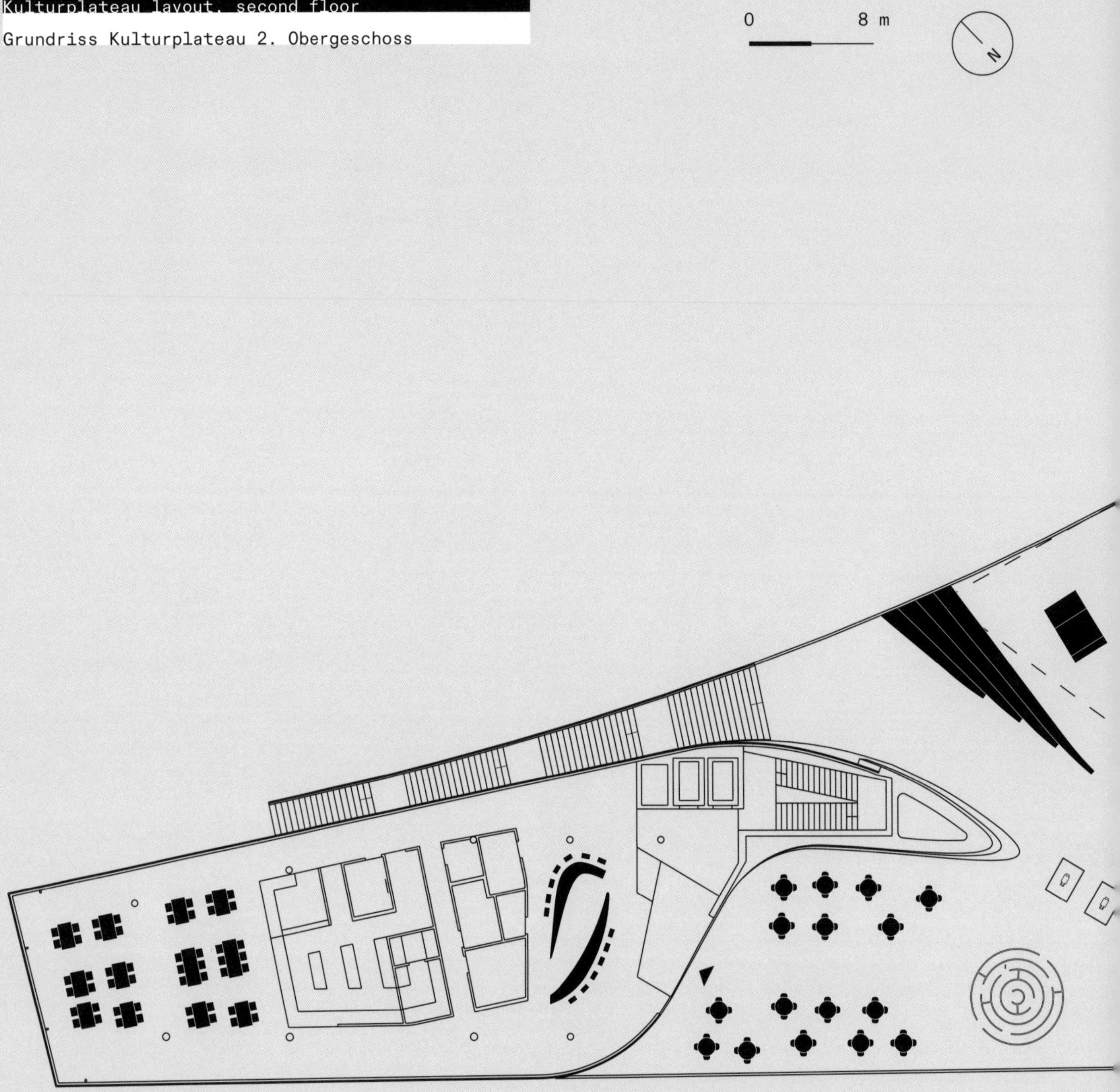

The Kulturplateau is a public space above the library and an essential part of an agreement between the investor and the municipality.

Das Kulturplateau ist ein öffentlicher Raum über der Bibliothek und ein wesentlicher Bestandteil einer Vereinbarung des Investors mit der Stadtverwaltung.

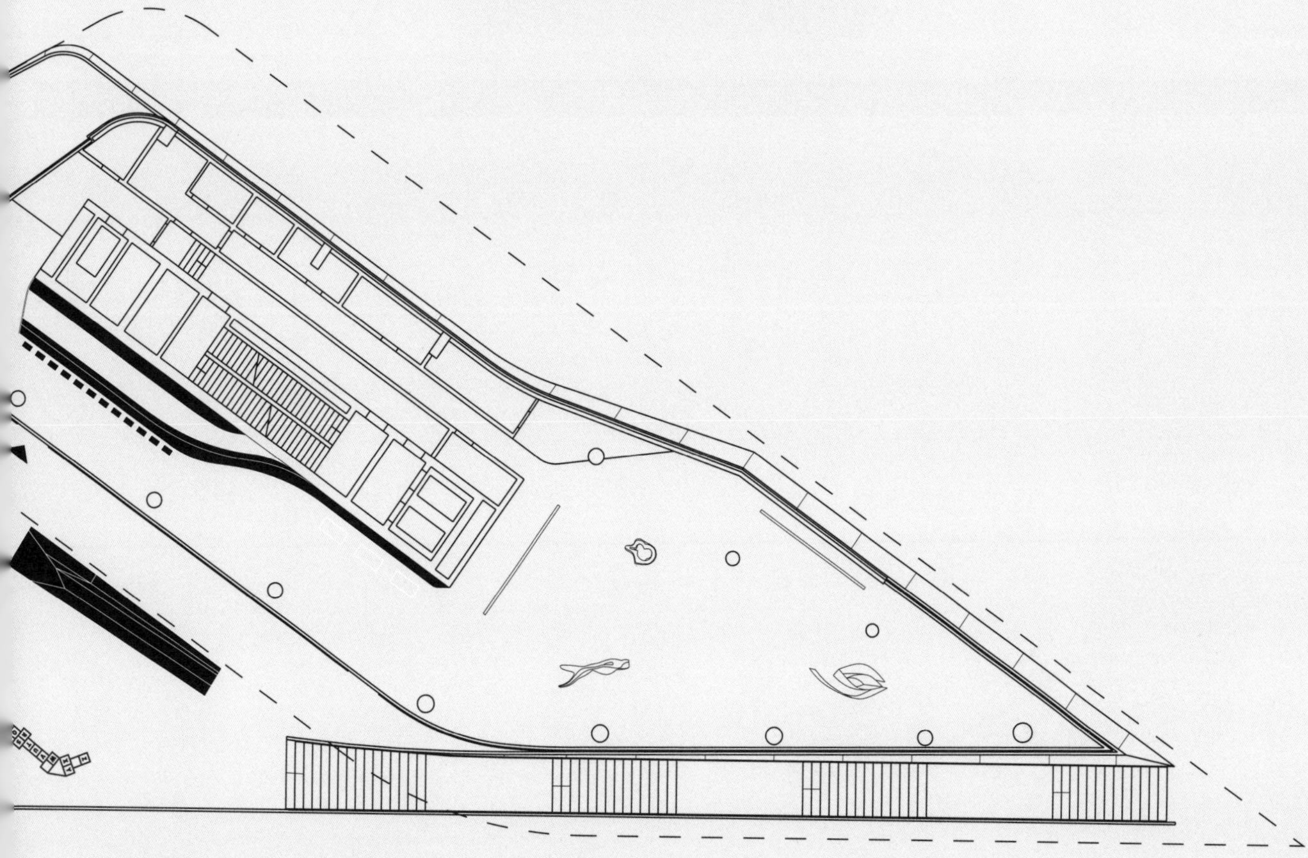

Area according to the requirements of the competition specification:

Fläche laut Raumprogramm Wettbewerbsausschreibung:

Exhibition space and restaurant / Ausstellungsfläche und Gastronomie:	1,000 m²
Privately financed housing / Frei finanziertes Wohnen:	2,500 m²
Student housing / Studentisches Wohnen:	7,000 m²
Offices / Büros:	1,500 m²
Retail and restaurants / Handel und Gastronomie:	4,000 m²
Total area / Gesamtfläche:	max. 16,000 m²

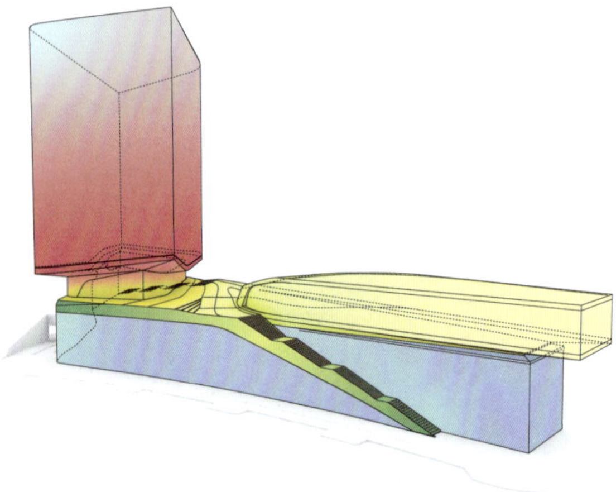

Area according to the submission plan:

Fläche laut Einreichplanung:

Residential / Wohnen:	14,300 m²
Public space, culture & restaurants / Öffentlicher Raum, Kultur und Gastronomie:	1,350 m²
Public library / Bibliothek:	4,800 m²
Total area / Gesamtfläche:	20,450 m²

Report of the Supervisory Department dated 20.12.2019, Zl. KA-05830/2019

In the concrete case of the object Amraser Straße 2-4 (Pema 2), the project applicant undertook to realise the construction project as (essentially) described as follows in the signed easement agreement:

"The project envisages a two- to, partly, three-storey base building above a three-storey underground car park. This base is to contain retailers, restaurants and service providers. The roof of the base will be accessible via two open stairs and can be used as a public terrace. This 'Cultural Plateau' provides public added value. It should be enriched and actively used in the form of an exhibition space, public uses and restaurants.

In addition to this, the project envisages the creation of ten storeys of apartments in the tower-like building."

Der Bericht der Kontrollabteilung vom 20.12.2019, Zl. KA-05830/2019

Im konkreten Fall des Objektes Amraser Straße 2-4 (Pema 2) verpflichtete sich die Projektwerberin zur Umsetzung eines im unterzeichneten Dienstbarkeitsvertrag (grundsätzlich) wie folgt beschriebenen Bauprojektes:

„Das Projekt sieht über einer dreigeschossigen Tiefgarage ein zwei- bis teilweise dreigeschossiges Sockelbauwerk vor. Im Sockelbauwerk sind Handels-, Gastronomie- und Dienstleistungsbetriebe vorgesehen. Das Dach des Sockels wird über zwei Freitreppen erschlossen und als öffentliche Terrasse angeboten. Dieses ‚Kulturplateau' bringt einen öffentlichen Mehrwert. Es soll durch einen Ausstellungsraum, öffentliche Nutzung und Gastronomie angereichert und aktiv genutzt werden.

[…]

Darüber hinaus sieht das Projekt im Bereich des turmartigen Gebäudes in zehn Geschossen Wohnungen vor."

Report of the Supervisory Department dated 27.08.2019, Zl. KA-03529/2019

The "Project Guarantee Contract", which takes the form of a private agreement, should guarantee that no project will be realised other than that jointly developed by the applicant and the building authorities. This joint project development will guarantee that the alterations in the development plan and, where applicable, zoning plan requested by the applicant for the easement are also in the public interest from the urban design and planning law perspectives. This guarantee is secured by the granting of the easement of a construction ban in the land register. In addition to this, the applicant for the easement undertakes to inform the Office for Urban Planning and Development and Integration without delay about all intended deviations and changes to the statutory approvals. Upon completion of the building, proof is to be provided that all key components of the project have been executed in line with the contract. In return, when the applicant for the easement has met all their obligations, Innsbruck City Council undertakes to delete the easement of the construction ban in the land register.

Der Bericht der Kontrollabteilung vom 27.08.2019, Zl. KA-03529/2019

Der „Projektsicherungsvertrag" in Form einer privatrechtlichen Vereinbarung soll garantieren, dass kein anderes als das gemeinsam von Bauwerber und Behörde entwickelte Projekt realisiert wird. Durch die gemeinsame Projektentwicklung wird gewährleistet, dass die seitens Dienstbarkeitsbestellerin angesuchte Änderung des Bebauungsplanes und ggf. der Flächenwidmung auch aus städtebaulicher und raumordnungsrechtlicher Sicht im öffentlichen Interesse ist. Die Sicherstellung erfolgt hierbei durch die grundbücherliche Einräumung der Dienstbarkeit eines Bauverbotes. Des Weiteren verpflichtet sich der Dienstbarkeitsbesteller, das Amt für Stadtplanung, Stadtentwicklung und Integration über sämtliche beabsichtigte Abweichungen und Abänderungen zu den behördlichen Genehmigungen unverzüglich zu verständigen. Nach Fertigstellung des Gebäudes ist ein Nachweis, dass alle wesentlichen Bestandteile des Projektes vertragskonform ausgeführt wurden, zu erbringen. Bei Erfüllung der vereinbarten Pflichten des Dienstbarkeitsbestellers verpflichtet sich die Stadt Innsbruck im Gegenzug zur grundbücherlichen Löschung der Dienstbarkeit des Bauverbotes.

ischia garage
Stadtbibliothek

INNS' BRUCK
stadtbibliothek

SBI	City Library Innsbruck	2018	Public library	Innsbruck Austria

PROJECT	TITLE	YEAR	SUBJECT	LOCATION

The realisation of the new city library in the base of P2 enhances the significance of an important public institution and creates an urban hinge that connects the neighbouring districts. The concept for Innsbruck's new city library treats the library itself as a public interior space and as a place of learning and coming together. Like the Viennese coffee house, the library of today can be seen as a consumption-free alternative setting, in which one can spend one's time with literature and newspapers and attend readings and discussions in a contemplative atmosphere. This trend is underpinned by the spatial concept, in which half of the space is dedicated to media and the other half is a place of relaxation and meeting. The result is a public interior zone that is as educational as it is highly integrative.

Mit dem Neubau der Stadtbibliothek in der Sockelzone des P2 gewinnt eine wichtige öffentliche Institution an Bedeutung und die angrenzenden Stadtteile erhalten eine Verbindung in Form eines städtebaulichen Gelenks. Das Konzept der neuen Stadtbibliothek Innsbruck versteht die Bibliothek als öffentlichen Innenraum, als Ort des Lernens und der Begegnung. Neben dem Wiener Kaffeehaus sind es heutzutage die Bibliotheken, die als konsumfreie Alternative das Verweilen mit Literatur und Zeitungen, den Besuch von Lesungen und Diskussionen in einer kontemplativen Atmosphäre ermöglichen. Diesem Trend liegt das Raumkonzept zugrunde, bei dem die eine Hälfte der Fläche für Medien, die andere Hälfte als Aufenthaltsraum genutzt wird. Es entsteht eine gleichzeitig bildungsorientierte und höchst integrative Innenraumzone für die Öffentlichkeit.

Innsbruck 2018
Ferrari, Martin Gostner, Bernhard Hetzenauer,
Klampfer, Gerald Nestler, Annelies Senfter,
Tinzl, Hannes Zebedin

First-floor library layout

Grundriss Erdgeschoss Bibliothek

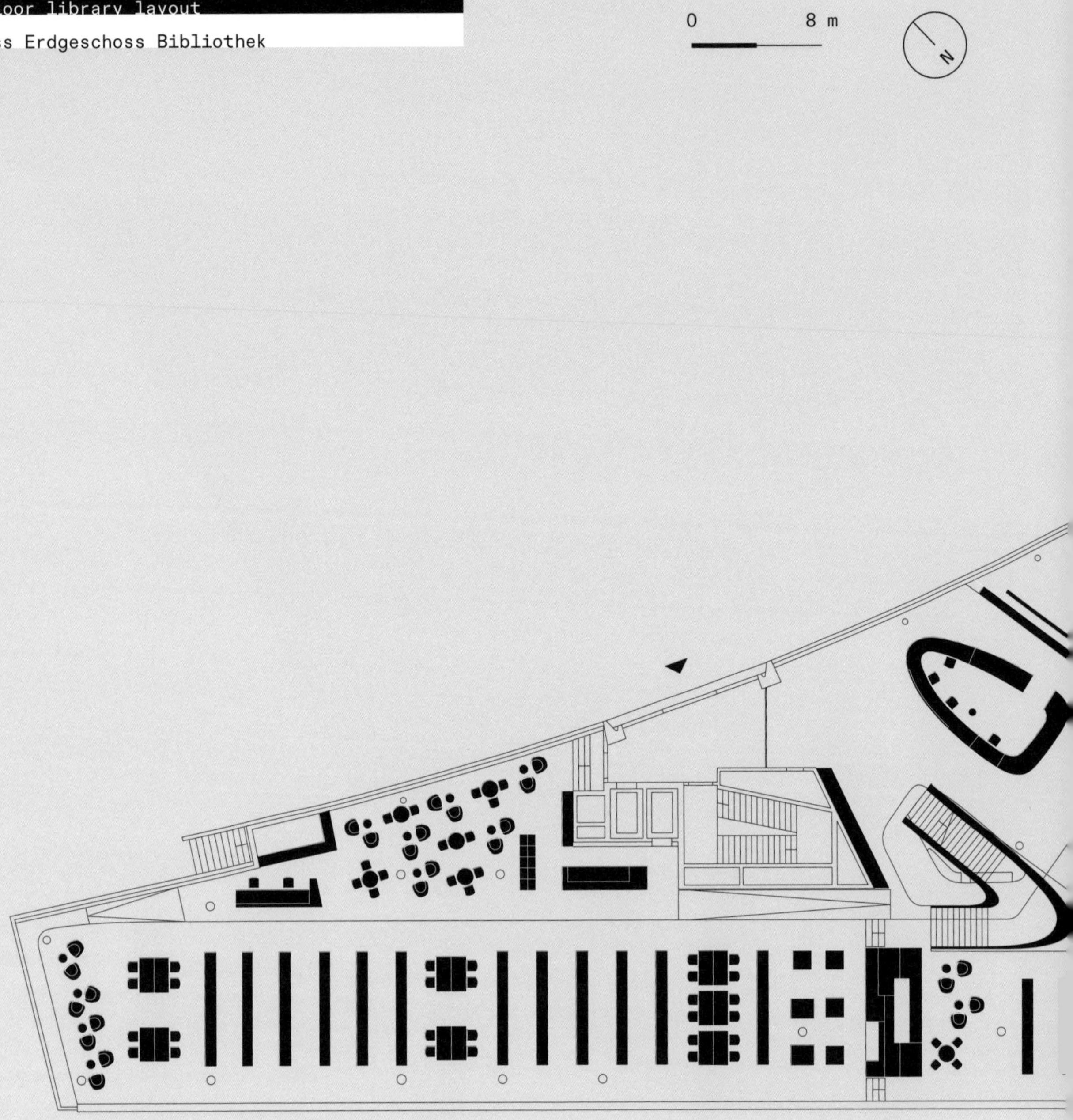

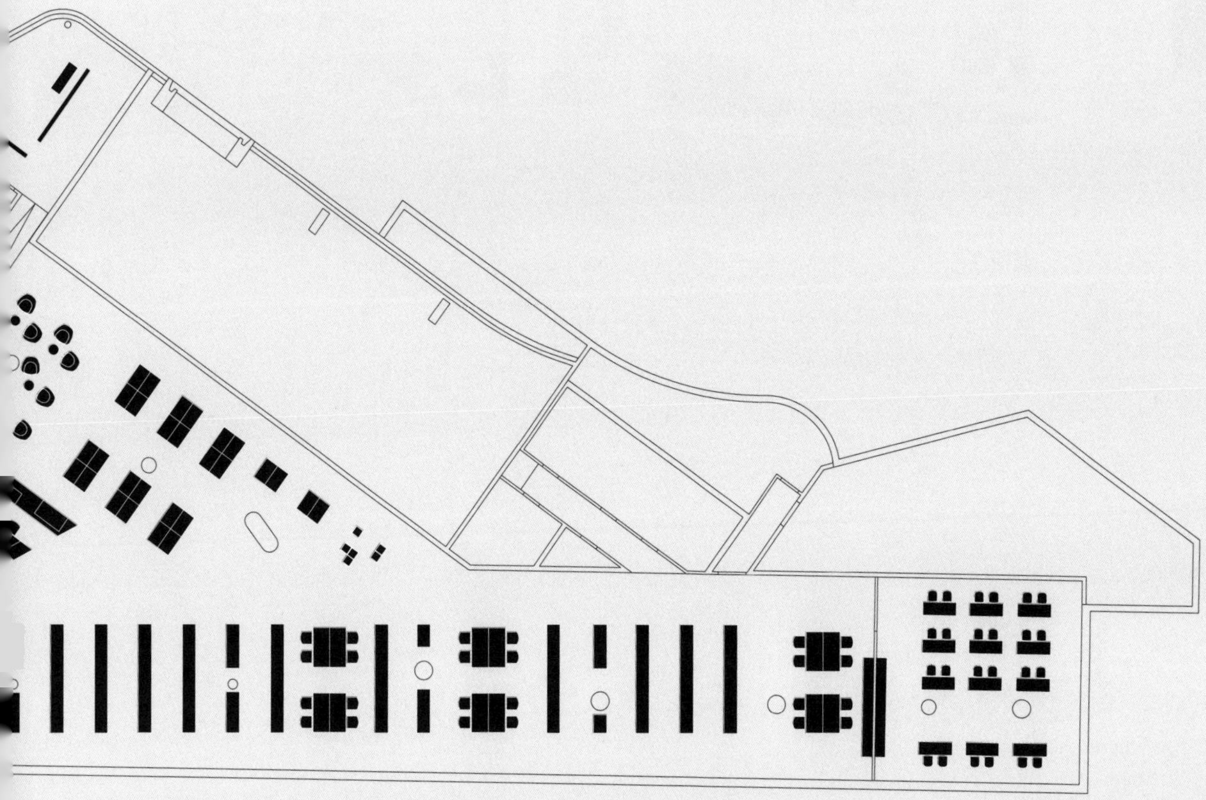

Perhaps the library is the only real freespace, for in being consistently public and personal at the same time, it expands the space between text and mind.

Vielleicht ist die Bibliothek der einzig wahre Freiraum, denn indem sie konsequent öffentlich und persönlich zugleich ist, erweitert sie den Raum zwischen Text und Geist.

m 6020

Staircase layout

Grundriss Treppe

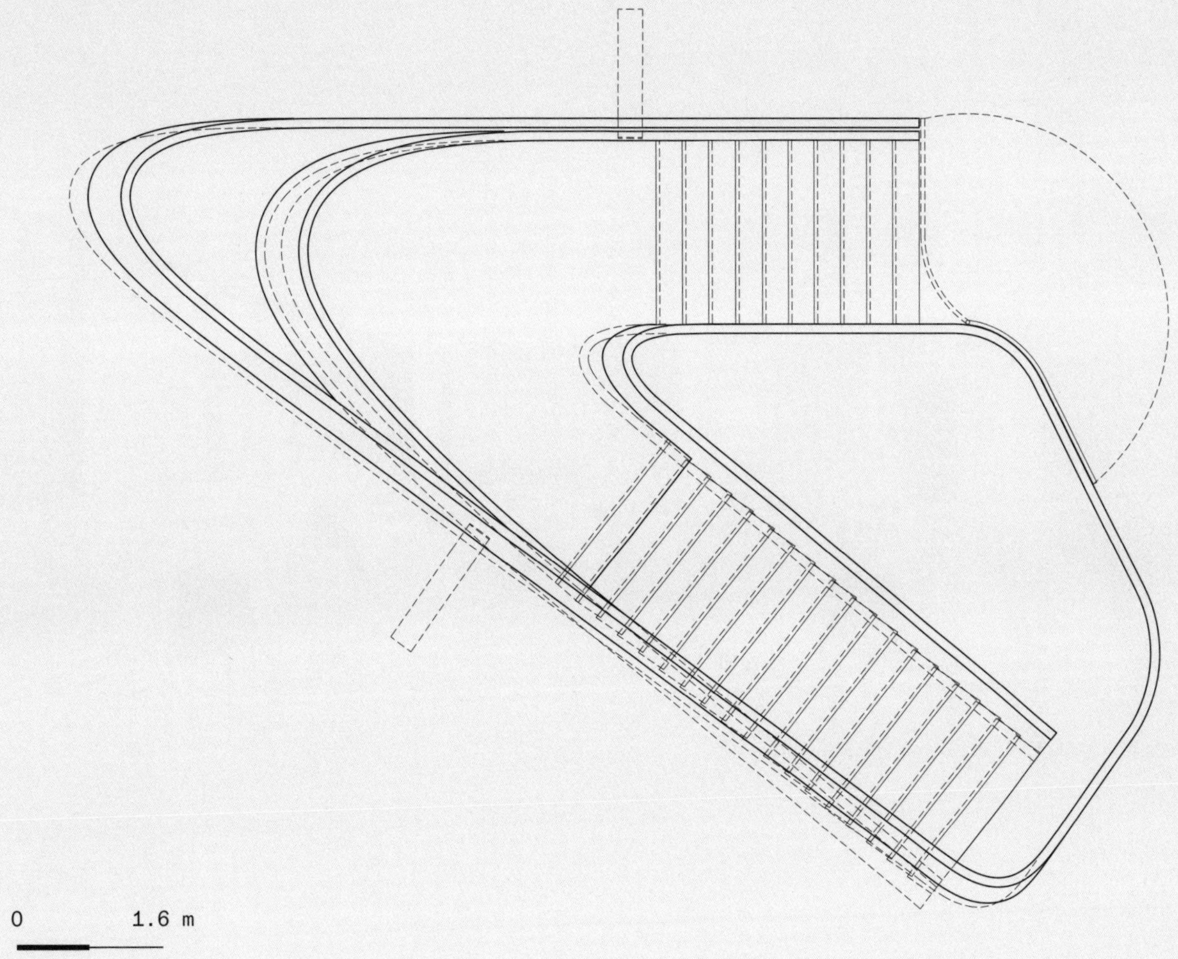

Comic
Graphic Novel

Ankäufe der Stadt Innsbruck 2018

Trurl is a bot, a virtual reader. When Trurl visits the website of the library, he reads author names, titles and keyword indexes. From these he writes new books.

Trurl ist ein Bot, ein virtueller Leser. Wenn Trurl die Internetseite der Stadtbibliothek Innsbruck besucht, liest er Autorennamen, Titel und Schlagwortverzeichnisse. Daraus schreibt er neuen Lesestoff.

A

WITH

Kathrin Aste

Corporate identity clearly plays a significant role in the positioning of a brand. It illustrates a company's self-image and attempts to develop a "sense of being us", which has an impact both internally and externally. The external impact of this self-image is also significantly influenced by the character of a company's architecture. This represents the company in the form of a building and positions it in a specific context.

The choice of differentiated architectural approaches seems to contradict the notion of corporate identity due to the fact that their recognition value can't be reduced to the repetition of eye-catching, signalling elements. Every building has a form and, accordingly, an identity that reflects its own contentual meaning. A culturally meaningful and sustainable architecture doesn't seek its meaning in the portfolio of a company but, rather, in the identity of the place that contributes to the shaping of its reality, history and atmosphere.

When designing a supermarket, it's impossible to escape the typology of the box. This can be contorted or rectangular, have a flat or a curved roof, columns or free spans, an underground garage or a surface car park, but, at the end of the day, the classic spatial container for exhibiting and storing food appears to be the most practical and efficient form. To a certain extent, this extremely simple and undefined space recalls the white cube that has been regarded as a perfect setting for exhibiting contemporary art since the 1920s. The presentation of food may be a less exclusive process but it's no less product-oriented and consumer-friendly. And yet, the greater the ability of this neutral space to present goods as effectively as possible, the less able it is to move us. Hence, after identifying the functional requirements of a market, the following question remains: How can one give a box a sense of identity?

In order to embrace and feel an association with a place, people require an emotional connection that is based on the identification of regional structures, archetypal patterns of memory and spatially recognisable analogies. Rural contexts in particular offer huge potential for establishing such a sense of identity. This creates an atmosphere that, in turn, enables people to consciously experience a space.

The concept behind the corporate design of the regional supermarket chain MPREIS is developed from a self-image that, rather than being based on a preconceived monotone appearance, consciously understands that architecture is a three-dimensional, spatial dialogue with one's customers and their environment.

BOX IDENTITY

Für die Positionierung einer Marke spielt die Corporate Identity zweifellos eine bedeutende Rolle. Sie verdeutlicht das Selbstverständnis eines Unternehmens und versucht, ein „Wir-Bewusstsein“ aufzubauen, das sowohl nach innen als auch nach außen wirkt. Die Außenwirkung dieses Selbstbildes hängt ebenso maßgeblich von der Beschaffenheit der Architektur ab. Sie repräsentiert ein Unternehmen in Form eines Gebäudes und verortet es in einem spezifischen Umfeld.

Differenzierte Architekturen scheinen im Widerspruch zur Idee der Corporate Identity zu stehen, zumal ihr Wiedererkennungswert nicht auf die Wiederholung plakativer Elemente mit Signalwirkung reduziert werden kann. Jedes Bauwerk hat eine Gestalt und dementsprechend auch eine Identität, die Bedeutungsinhalte widerspiegelt. Eine kulturell sinnvolle und nachhaltige Architektur sucht ihre Bedeutung nicht primär im Portfolio eines Unternehmens, sondern in der Identität des Ortes, dessen Realität, Geschichte und Atmosphäre sie mitgestaltet.

Beim Entwurf eines Supermarktes führt kein Weg an der Typologie der Box vorbei. Sie kann verzogen oder rechtwinkelig, mit geradem oder geschwungenem Dach, mit Stützen oder freitragend, mit Tiefgarage oder mit Parkplatz sein, schlussendlich scheint der klassische Raumbehälter für das Ausstellen und Lagern von Lebensmitteln die praktikabelste und effizienteste Form zu sein. Der möglichst einfache und undefinierte Raum erinnert mitunter an den White Cube, den weißen Würfel, der seit den 1920er-Jahren als perfekter Ausstellungraum für zeitgenössische Kunst gilt. Das Präsentieren von Lebensmitteln mag weniger exklusiv sein, aber nicht weniger produktorientiert und rezipientenfreundlich. Aber so sehr dieser neutrale Raum die Fähigkeit hat, die Ware so wirkungsvoll wie möglich anzubieten, so wenig vermag uns die Box zu berühren. Demnach stellt sich nach dem Anerkennen der funktionalen Anforderungen an einen Markt die Frage: Wie verleiht man einer Box Identität?

Damit Menschen einen Ort annehmen und sich mit ihm verbunden fühlen, bedarf es einer emotionalen Bindung, die auf der Identifikation regionaler Strukturen, archetypischer Erinnerungsmuster und räumlich wiedererkennbarer Analogien beruht. Insbesondere der landschaftliche Kontext verfügt im Sinne der Identitätsbildung über ein großes Potenzial. Dies schafft eine Atmosphäre, die dem Menschen das bewusste Erleben eines Raums ermöglicht.

Das Konzept des Corporate Design des Nahversorgers MPREIS beruht auf einem Selbstbild, das nicht auf ein vorgefasstes monotones Bild baut, sondern sich bewusst ist, dass Architektur einen dreidimensionalen, räumlichen Dialog mit den Kund*innen und deren Umfeld darstellt.

MPREIS

MPV	MPREIS Volders	2022	Supermarket	Volders Austria
PROJECT	TITLE	YEAR	SUBJECT	LOCATION

Volders is a Tyrolean community with rural surroundings and a village structure. The spatial quality of the locality is fragile and requires cautious land-use planning. This project responds to the challenge of sustainably integrating the relatively large area of a supermarket into the local context by combining this with housing. The result is that neither of the two functions dominates. Apparent contradictions such as public and private, serial and specific, minimalist and comfortable are addressed holistically in a solution that seeks to minimise the consumption of both land and resources.

Volders ist eine Gemeinde in Tirol mit ländlicher Umgebung und dörflicher Struktur. Die räumliche Qualität der Ortschaft ist fragil und abhängig von einer umsichtigen Flächenwidmung. Der Herausforderung, die verhältnismäßig große Fläche eines Supermarktes nachhaltig in den Ortskontext zu integrieren, begegnet das Projekt, indem es einen Wohnbau mit einem Lebensmittelmarkt verbindet. Dabei dominiert weder das eine noch das andere. Scheinbar Widersprüchliches wie öffentlich und privat, seriell und spezifisch, minimalistisch und gemütlich werden bodensparend und ressourcenschonend miteinander verhandelt.

Tyrol Regional Planning Law – TROG 2022 § 48a
Special areas for commercial companies

(4) In the interests of guaranteeing forms of development that use land sparingly, and if compatible with the objectives of the public planning guidelines, multi-storey development and the multiple use of the relevant areas of land are to be ensured by means of appropriate provisions in the zoning and development plans.

Tiroler Raumordnungsgesetz – TROG 2022 § 48a
Sonderflächen für Handelsbetriebe

(4) Im Interesse der Gewährleistung einer Boden sparenden Bebauung sind, soweit dies mit den Zielen der örtlichen Raumordnung vereinbar ist, eine mehrgeschossige Bebauung und eine Mehrfachnutzung der betroffenen Grundflächen durch entsprechende Festlegungen des Flächenwidmungsplanes und des Bebauungsplanes sicherzustellen.

MEHRWEG

RAUCH
EIS TEE
bravo
bravo
ARANCIA
ARANCIA
KIDNEY BOHNEN
Traube Saft
Milde Apfel
Orange Saft
Pink Grapefruit
COCO drink

MPW	MPREIS Weer	2017	Supermarket	Weer Austria
PROJECT	TITLE	YEAR	SUBJECT	LOCATION

The supermarket in Weer underlines the environmental commitment of the local chain MPREIS by taking a holistic approach to sustainability. The passive building picks up on specific characteristics of the surrounding landscape and vegetation, such as the textures of the fields, grasses and trees, and translates these into both surface and space. The building is embedded in the greenery of the fields, while the facade of polished stainless steel panels reflects the natural context and the internal courtyard brings nature into the supermarket in the form of a tree that establishes a rich contrast with the trunk-like concrete columns.

Der Supermarkt in Weer unterstreicht das Engagement des Nahversorgers MPREIS für Umweltbewusstsein und verfolgt dabei einen ganzheitlichen Ansatz von Nachhaltigkeit. Das Passivhaus greift die lokalen Besonderheiten der umgebenden Landschaft und deren Vegetation, wie die Beschaffenheit der Felder, Gräser und Bäume, auf, welche in Fläche und Raum übersetzt werden. Das Gebäude ist in das Grün der Felder eingebettet, die Metallfassade aus polierten Edelstahlplatten spiegelt den natürlichen Kontext wider, der Innenhof mit Baum holt die Natur in den Markt und steht im Kontrast zu den Baumstützen aus Beton.

Even if called a passive house, architecture takes an active role to negotiate specific regional potentials with global considerations.

Wenn auch als Passivhaus bezeichnet, so übernimmt die Architektur eine aktive Rolle, um spezifische regionale Potenziale mit globalen Überlegungen zu vereinbaren.

Schwechater
RADLER
STIBITZER
DESPERADOS

SUPER

MPS	MPREIS Sölden	2022	Supermarket	Sölden Austria

The MPREIS in Sölden is an Alpine version of the MPREIS Weer. Once again, the aim of the design is to integrate the store as naturally as possible into its close surroundings. The flat green fields are replaced by steep rocky slopes, which are architecturally translated into the interior. In accordance with the characteristic landscape surroundings, the building is organised vertically. The storage, parking deck, market and roofscape are layered on top of each other, consuming little footprint. The reflective box tells about the characteristic landscape of the valley in the change of the four seasons.

Der MPREIS in Sölden ist eine alpine Variante des MPREIS in Weer. Auch hier ist das Ziel der Gestaltung, den Markt möglichst selbstverständlich in die unmittelbare Umgebung zu integrieren. Anstelle der flachen grünen Felder treten steile felsige Hänge, die sich architektonisch übersetzt im Innenraum wiederfinden. Entsprechend der charakteristischen landschaftlichen Umgebung organisiert sich das Bauwerk vertikal. Das Lager, das Parkdeck, der Markt und die Dachlandschaft werden übereinandergeschichtet und verbrauchen nur wenig Grundfläche. Die reflektierende Box erzählt von der charakteristischen Landschaft des Tals im Wandel der vier Jahreszeiten.

MPREIS MPREIS

1.49
TOPERCZER

NIMBLE CURVES

ENIGMATIC SOLIDS

AND

Oliver Domeisen

The slow descent by aircraft into the wide trench of the Inn Valley has an unnerving and sublime effect on the traveller. When minutes ago picturesque high-altitude views of the Tyrolian Alps, all sugar-coated peaks and misty valleys, were safely kept at a distance beyond the porthole frame, a menacing mass of craggy rock – a looming tidal wave of stone – now suddenly seems to surge upward all around us. The jagged celestial horizon ascends relentlessly out of view, plunging us inexorably into the gaping jaws of the shadowed vale below. Such would be the account of my journey were I inclined towards a Ruskinian romantic view.

If, on the other hand, I attempted to observe what would be very familiar scenery through the trained eyes of LAAC, then a very different picture should emerge. As the visor of my VR space helmet lowers with a satisfying purring sound, and the heads-up display beams brightly into my retina, this mountainous topography dissolves into a glowing gossamer veil of grids, quadmeshes and point clouds. Messy mineral solids give way to intricately tesselated surfaces, delicately woven lines and clouds of vaporous particles. The effortlessly dematerialised mass now sheds its geological, historical and mythological weight and remodels itself as a digital high-altitude plane of timeless clarity and pure reason, a billowing Shangrila where shimmering arrays of Alpine power plants (SDI* 2012–2015) glisten beyond lost horizons.

LAAC's technical dexterity, as much as poetry, in using pattern and geometry to reimagine landscape is never reductive. Their redrawing of landscape (NPO* 2012–2017), as a form of artistic abstraction, allows for the human gesture – or rather the gestural expression of humanity – to become inscribed within the landscape as a form of "generative synthesis".

The observation platform above the Stubai Glacier (TOP* 2009) is a mere bundle of elegant lines; lines that trace the swift movement of a hand that draws a curve in space, but also topographical lines that emerge seamlessly from their surroundings like rogue cartographic contours. The platform complements the cliff edge in the same manner as head-clouds form along mountain crests. From afar its Corten swords resemble strands of russet hair, maybe plucked from the head of Botticelli's Venus and drifting on an upwind, before getting caught within the cracks of the rugged ridge. This achingly beautiful prosthesis for the tourist gaze then aligns with Renaissance-scholar Aby Warburg's notion of *bewegtes Beiwerk*. Like Botticelli's painted fluttering hair and cloth, the platform operates as a sort of ornament that reframes, destabilises and animates the otherwise stable visual environment it inhabits. In LAAC's process the landscape is not merely being inscribed with form, but the landscape itself is being rewritten as an architectural figure emerging or dissipating through faint lines in the snow.

LAAC's command of curves is simply spectacular; sometimes they are held in perfect tension, like the spherical segment inserted into Josef Hoffmann's Austrian Venice Biennale Pavilion (VAP* 2018), or their splaying bundles of steps along the shores of the Danube near Vienna (CCN* 2018–2021). Alternatively, at their Landhausplatz in Innsbruck (LHP* 2010) and in their design for a Norwegian ski jump (HKB* 2007), the curvature choreographs human bodies into a permanent state of precarious acceleration. LAAC's movements here become a balletic expression of perfect control, able to withstand even the most improbable centrifugal forces. The momentum of their particular curves manifests subtle asymmetries and deviations, like a carefully judged backhand slice across the tennis court; perfection as a result of endless training and refinement.

We are reminded of a fellow master of curvature, who shared similar Alpine inclinations: Carlo Mollino. An architect, skiing instructor and gifted photographer, Mollino documented the elegant movement of Austrian skiing-ace Leo Gasperl in the 1930s. He then published his own *Introduction to Downhill Skiing* (1950) before embarking on the construction of *Casa Cattaneo* above Lago Maggiore (1952–1953). The building reverberates with a profound comprehension of such agile speed. The articulation of its structural undercroft indeed echoes through the dynamism of elements in LAAC's own Pema 2 development (PMA* 2015–2019) in Innsbruck. Here, at a junction for the civic life of the city, heavy masses seemingly begin to levitate and tall volumes race around sharp bends. In numerous designs LAAC seize upon particular expressions of differing dynamics: those of the architect's hand, those of enhanced physical propulsion, and even those of geological convulsion.

To return to the romantic view of John Ruskin for a moment: on his trips to the Alps he indeed observed such correlations between natural forces and curvature and declared them to be a core characteristic of nature itself. In his illustration titled *Abstract Lines* (Plate VII, *The Stones of Venice*, Vol. II, 1851) Ruskin identified elongated gestural curves as a core aesthetic of the Alpine landscape, apparent in glaciers, turbulent clouds and geological strata. He concludes: "The very glory of a mountain is in the revolutions which raised it into power, and the forces which are striking it into ruin."

Albrecht Dürer, *Melencolia I*

It would be capricious to frame LAAC's work as narrowly contextual in terms of its location or geography, rather than in terms of global and local architectural currents over the last thirty years. It may nevertheless prove a fruitful experiment to pull focus on the practice's particular setting. The now familiar mountain range that forms the Inn Valley makes an appearance in another intriguing LAAC design. The underwhelming setting for the project is a prosaic car park on the edge of an unremarkable village east of Innsbruck. A generic and familiar context for any suburban general store. But even here LAAC have managed to augment the banal to the architecturally sublime, going above and beyond the client MPREIS's commendable ambition for placemaking through unique architectural solutions, where each store should be an

R.P. Cuff after / nach John Ruskin, *Abstract Lines*

idiosyncratic reflection of its locality (MPW* 2017).

Seen from the car park the MPREIS store in Weer does not appear primarily as a container of merchandise, but as a concrete plinth. The low-set box forms a podium for the snow-capped peaks in the background, now isolating and framing that particular part of the landscape as if it were a discrete sculptural object. On approach the lateral and back facades, sheathed in stainless steel, furthermore mirror the surroundings, forever expanding the verdant fields and Alpine horizons. The polished and gently ridged metal panels relinquish simple doubling in favour of complex distortion. When observed at an angle the reflected landscape becomes subject to a gradual disintegration of the image, evocative of a Gerhard Richter-esque painterly, rather than a photorealist, sensibility. A naturally planted and glazed internal courtyard, a green-tinted window and illustrations of animals as point clouds on the walls produce further reworkings of the "natural" prototype, engaging artistically with the consumables on display.

The most striking examples of such versions of synthetic nature are surely what the architects have called "tree columns": double- or triple-pronged tessellated volumes featuring polygonal facets. In terms of scale and their structural function they certainly act as arboreal tropes, referring to the tree as a structural metaphor; yet they could not be further removed from previous attempts to bring the tree inside a store, as for example in SITE/James Wines' famous design for the Best Products Company store in Richmond VA (USA 1980). Rather than representing actual trees LAAC's bifurcating abstract forms are deeply mysterious and ambivalent objects.

In one of Albrecht Dürer's three master engravings, *Melencolia I* (1514), a winged figure holding a caliper (or compass) is contemplating a truncated rhombohedron, the so-called *Dürer Solid*. According to the Renaissance imagination melancholy was associated with artistic imagination, while geometry – here represented by various tools – was the one liberal art facilitating artistic creation. The *Dürer Solid*, reimagined by Alberto Giacometti as a fulcrum of artistic abstraction in his sculpture *Cube* (1934), remains one of Western art's most mysterious and contested objects. Is it pure geometry, a platonic solid, where all vertices are located on a sphere? Is it simply the representation of a crystal structure, such as that of rhombohedral calcite? In my own melancholic contemplation of LAAC's *Solids* such considerations fade into the background. Here architecture as inherently the most abstract of all the arts has produced objects that refuse singular interpretation. We may simply want to see trees holding up the canopy. Or are these maybe hand gestures of a three-finger oath swearing allegiance to an unshakable faith in architecture? Are they crystalline stalagmites growing within a cavernous accretion of consumerism, now alluding to Alpine mineralogy and a famous local crystal-manufacturing industry?

Surely they are all and none of those things. What

matters is that these mysterious objects are able to communicate with the physical and non-physical world that surrounds them in interesting ways. And in an essential way they tell us something fundamental about the use of geometry and abstraction in the work of LAAC as a whole. Their understanding of geometry in its relation to the art of architecture seems to concur with that of Ruskin, as he writes in his first-ever published text: "[Geometry] is not merely a science of the rule and compass, it does not consist only in the observation of just rule, or of fair proportion: it is, or ought to be, a science of feeling more than of rule, a ministry to the mind, more than to the eye."[1]

Der träge Sinkflug in die breite Furche des Inntals wirkt auf Passagier*innen zugleich beängstigend und sublim. Noch vor wenigen Minuten schien das malerische Höhenpanorama der Tiroler Alpen, schienen all seine gezuckerten Berggipfel und dunstigen Täler vom Rahmen des Flugzeugfensters auf sichere Distanz gehalten. Doch plötzlich scheint sich eine bedrohliche Masse schroffer Felsen zu erheben, steinerne Flutwellen türmen sich immer höher um uns herum. Der zerklüftete Himmelshorizont übersteigt unaufhaltsam unser Sichtfeld und wir stürzen unerbittlich in den tiefen Schlund des schattigen Tals. So läse sich wohl mein Reisebericht, wäre ich ein Romantiker in den Fußstapfen John Ruskins. Würde ich jedoch versuchen, durch das geschulte Auge von LAAC das ihnen äußerst vertraute Panorama zu betrachten, dann würde wohl ein ganz anderes Bild entstehen. Wenn sich das Visier meines VR-Astronautenhelms angenehm schnurrend senkt und sich das helle Heads-Up-Display in meine Netzhaut brennt, dann verwandelt sich diese Gebirgstopografie in einen glühenden, hauchdünnen Schleier aus Gittern, Netzen und Punktwolken. Ungeordnete mineralische Körper weichen minutiös gefelderten Flächen, fein gewebten Linien und sich zu

Dunstwolken gruppierenden Partikeln. Die mühelos entmaterialisierte Masse entledigt sich so ihres geologischen, historischen und mythologischen Gewichts und erfindet sich neu als eine digitale Hochebene von zeitloser Klarheit und reiner Vernunft, ein wogendes Shangri-La, in dem schimmernde Scharen alpiner Kraftwerke (SDP*, 2012–2015) jenseits verlorener Horizonte funkeln.

Die technische wie auch poetische Geschicklichkeit, mit der LAAC unter Verwendung von Mustern und Geometrien Landschaften neu erfinden, wirkt niemals reduzierend. Ihr Überzeichnen der Landschaft (NPO*, 2012–2017), als künstlerische Abstraktion, erlaubt es der menschlichen Geste – oder vielmehr einem gestischen Ausdruck des Menschseins –, sich in Form einer „generativen Synthese" in die Landschaft einzuschreiben.

Die Aussichtsplattform oberhalb des Stubaier Gletschers (TOP*, 2009) ist lediglich ein Bündel aus eleganten Linien; Linien, die der flüchtigen Bewegung einer Hand nachspüren, welche eine Kurve in den Raum zeichnet; aber auch topografische Linien, die nahtlos aus ihrer Umgebung entspringen wie ausbrechende Höhenkurven. Die Plattform harmoniert mit der Felskante in gleicher Weise wie Kopfwolken mit den Bergkämmen, entlang derer sie sich bilden. Aus der Ferne gleichen ihre Schwerter aus Cortenstahl rostbraunen Haarsträhnen – möglicherweise gewonnen vom Haupt der Botticelli-*Venus* und vom Aufwind hochgetragen –, die sich nun in den Rissen des zerklüfteten Grats verfangen haben. Diese leidenschaftlich schöne Prothese für die Sicht der Tourist*innen entspricht somit dem von Renaissance-Autorität Aby Warburg geprägten Begriff des *bewegten Beiwerks*. Analog zu Botticellis malerisch flatternden Haaren und Tüchern fungiert die Plattform als eine Art Ornament, das den ansonsten statischen Bildraum neu definiert, destabilisiert und bewegt. Im künstlerischen Prozess von LAAC wird der Landschaft nicht nur eine Form eingeschrieben; die Landschaft selbst wird als architektonische Figur umrissen, die in schummrigen Linien aus dem Schnee empordringt oder sich darin verflüchtigt.

Wie LAAC Kurven zu meistern wissen, ist spektakulär. Manchmal werden diese in einer perfekten Spannung gehalten, wie etwa beim Einfügen eines Kugelsegments in den österreichischen Pavillon von Josef Hoffmann in Venedig (VAP*, 2018) oder bei den sich spreizenden Bündeln von Stufen entlang des Donauufers bei Wien (CCV*, 2018–2021). Ganz anders agiert die Kurvatur auf ihrem Landhausplatz in Innsbruck (LHP*, 2010) und in ihrem Entwurf für eine norwegische Skisprungschanze (HKB*, 2007). Da wird sie zu einer Choreografie, die den menschlichen Körper in einen permanenten Zustand prekärer Beschleunigung versetzt. LAACs Dynamik wird hier zu einem balletthaften Ausdruck von perfekter Kontrolle, fähig, sogar den gewaltigsten Zentrifugalkräften zu widerstehen. Der Schwung ihrer besonderen Kurven offenbart subtile Asymmetrien und Abweichungen, gleich einem sorgsam ausgerichteten Rückhandslice quer über den Tennisplatz; Perfektion als Ergebnis von unaufhörlichem Training und Finesse.

Dies erinnert an einen verwandten Meister der Kurvatur mit ähnlich alpinen Neigungen: Carlo Mollino. Mollino – Architekt, Skilehrer und begnadeter Fotograf – dokumentierte die eleganten Schwünge der österreichischen Skilegende Leo Gasperl in den 1930er-Jahren. Anschließend veröffentlichte er seine *Einführung in den Abfahrtslauf* (1950), bevor er oberhalb des Lago Maggiore die Casa Cattaneo (1952–1953) erschuf. Der Bau reflektiert ein tief greifendes Verständnis solch gewandter Schnelligkeit. Die dynamische Artikulation seiner Tragstruktur klingt nach in Gestaltungselementen von LAACs Pema-2-Gebäude (PMA*, 2015–2019) in Innsbruck. Hier, an einem Knotenpunkt urbanen Lebens, beginnen schwere Massen, scheinbar zu schweben, und in die Höhe ragende Volumen rasen um scharfe Kurven. In diversen Entwürfen greifen LAAC bestimmte Ausdrucksformen unterschiedlicher Dynamiken auf: jene der flüchtigen Handgeste der Architekt*innen, jene der beschleunigten Propulsion von Objekten, ja selbst jene geologischer Konvulsionen.

Um für einen Moment zu John Ruskins romantischer Sichtweise zurückzukehren: Auf seinen Reisen durch die Alpen erkannte dieser wahrlich Zusammenhänge zwischen Naturkräften und

Kurvatur und beschrieb die Kurve als Kernmerkmal der Natur selbst. In seiner Illustration *Abstract Lines* (Tafel VII, Die Steine von Venedig, 1851) identifizierte Ruskin tatsächlich elongierte gestische Kurven als ästhetisches Hauptmerkmal der alpinen Landschaft, erkennbar in Gletschern, turbulenten Wolken und geologischen Schichtungen. Er kam zu folgendem Schluss: „Die wahre Pracht eines Berges liegt in der Umwälzung, welche ihn emporhob, und den Kräften, welche ihn wieder in den Abgrund stürzen."

Es wäre wohl eher kapriziös, die Arbeiten von LAAC als streng kontextuell im Hinblick auf Lage oder Geografie anstelle von globalen und lokalen architektonischen Strömungen der letzten 30 Jahre zu definieren. Dennoch könnte es sich als produktives Experiment erweisen, das besondere landschaftliche Umfeld des Architekturbüros für einmal in den Fokus zu rücken. Die uns nun schon vertraute Bergkette, die das Inntal formt, tritt nochmals auf in einem weiteren spannungsvollen Entwurf von LAAC. Die wenig beeindruckende Kulisse für das Projekt ist ein prosaischer Parkplatz am Rande eines unscheinbaren Dorfes östlich von Innsbruck, ein gewöhnlicher und gewohnter Kontext für einen vorstädtischen Supermarkt. Aber selbst hier ist es LAAC gelungen, das Banale zum architektonisch Erhabenen zu sublimieren. Dabei übertreffen sie sogar die bereits lobenswerten Bestrebungen der Bauherrschaft (MPREIS), durch einzigartige architektonische Lösungen einen Ort zu schaffen, wobei jedes Geschäft zum unverwechselbaren Ausdruck seiner Lokalität werden soll (MPW*, 2017).

Vom Parkplatz aus betrachtet, erscheint der MPREIS-Bau nicht in erster Linie als ein Behälter von Waren, sondern als betoniertes Postament. Die gedrungene Box bildet ein Podest für die schneebedeckten Gipfel im Hintergrund, isoliert und überhöht diesen Teil der Landschaft, so als wäre er ein autonomes skulpturales Objekt. Nähert man sich dem Gebäude, spiegeln die mit Edelstahl verkleideten seitlichen und rückwärtigen Fassaden die Umgebung wider und weiten die saftgrünen Felder und alpinen Horizonte ins Unendliche aus. Anstelle einer einfachen Doppelung produzieren die polierten und fein gerippten Metallpaneele komplexe Verwischungen. Aus der Schräge betrachtet, löst sich das Bild einer gespiegelten Landschaft sukzessive auf, was eher an die malerische Sensibilität eines Gerhard Richter als an Fotorealismus erinnert. Ein natürlich bepflanzter und verglaster Innenhof, ein grün getöntes Fenster und Zeichnungen von Tieren als Punktwolken an den Wänden ergeben weitere Umarbeitungen des Prototyps „Natur" und interagieren auf kunstvolle Art mit den zur Schau gestellten Waren. Die markantesten Beispiele solcher Versionen synthetischer Natur sind wohl die *Baum-Säulen*, wie sie von den Architekt*innen bezeichnet werden: zwei- oder dreizinkige, tesselierte und polygonal facettierte Volumen. Bezogen auf ihren Maßstab und ihre Tragfunktion fungieren diese gewiss als Baumtrope, indem sie auf den Baum als strukturelle Metapher verweisen. Allerdings könnten sie nicht weiter entfernt sein von früheren Versuchen, den Baum ins Geschäft zu bringen, wie zum Beispiel der im berühmten Entwurf von SITE / James Wines für die Best-Products-Company-Filiale in Richmond, Virginia (USA, 1980). Die sich gabelnden abstrakten Formen von LAAC sind nicht wirklich ein Versuch, Bäume darzustellen; sie sind zutiefst mysteriöse und ambivalente Objekte.

Auf *Melencolia I* (1514), einem der drei Meisterstiche von Albrecht Dürer, hält eine Figur mit Flügeln einen Zirkel (oder Kompass) in der Hand und betrachtet ein abgestumpftes Rhomboeder, das sogenannte Dürer-Polyeder. In der Vorstellungswelt der Renaissance wurde Melancholie mit künstlerischer Imagination assoziiert, während die Geometrie – hier durch verschiedene Werkzeuge dargestellt – die freie Kunst war, welche das künstlerische Schaffen erst ermöglichte. Das Dürer-Polyeder, von Alberto Giacometti in seiner Skulptur *Cube* (1934) als ein Dreh- und Angelpunkt künstlerischer Abstraktion neu konzipiert, bleibt bis heute eines der rätselhaftesten und umstrittensten Objekte der westlichen Kunst. Ist es reine Geometrie, ein platonischer Körper, dessen Eckpunkte sich alle auf derselben Umkugel befinden? Ist es einfach die Darstellung einer kristallinen Struktur, wie etwa jene des rhomboedrischen Kalzits? Bei meiner eigenen melancholischen Kontemplation der Polyeder von LAAC entschwinden solche Überlegungen in den Hintergrund. Hier hat die Architektur, von Natur aus die abstrakteste aller Künste, Objekte hervorgebracht, die sich einer singulären Interpretation verweigern. Wir möchten vielleicht einfach nur Bäume sehen, die eine Decke stützen. Oder sind dies vielleicht Handgesten, die mit hochgehaltenen drei Fingern einen Treueeid auf den unerschütterlichen Glauben an die Architektur schwören? Sind es kristallene Stalagmiten, die in den Höhlensystemen der Konsumkultur wachsen und nun sowohl auf die Mineralogie der Alpen als auch auf eine berühmte hiesige Kristallproduktionsindustrie anspielen?

Sie sind wohl alles und nichts von alledem. Worauf es ankommt, ist, dass diese rätselhaften Objekte in der Lage sind, mit der physischen und nicht physischen Welt um sie herum auf interessante Art zu kommunizieren. Und auf bedeutsame Art erzählen sie uns etwas Wesentliches über den Gebrauch von Geometrie und Abstraktion in den Arbeiten von LAAC insgesamt. Ihr Verständnis von Geometrie in Beziehung zur Kunstform Architektur scheint mit jenem von Ruskin übereinzustimmen, wie er es in seinem ersten je veröffentlichten Text beschreibt: „[Die Geometrie] ist nicht bloß eine Wissenschaft von Lineal und Zirkel; sie besteht nicht allein in der Einhaltung einfacher Regeln oder schöner Proportion: sie ist, oder sollte vielmehr eine Wissenschaft des Gefühls als eine der Regel sein, eher ein Dienst am Geiste als am Auge."[1]

1 "The Poetry of Architecture; or, The Architecture of the Nations of Europe Considered in Its Association with Natural Scenery and National Character", in: Loudon's Architectural Magazine, 1837.

Oliver Domeisen is a London-based Swiss architect, ornamentalist, curator and academic. He is a lecturer in history & theory at UCL Bartlett, was a guest lecturer at the Institute for Experimental Architecture at the University of Innsbruck, guest professor at the Academy of Fine Arts Vienna, from 2001 to 2013 Unit Master and from 2013 to 2017 member of the Board of Directors at the Architectural Association London. Previously he was curator of contemporary architecture and urban design at the V&A Museum, project architect for Zaha Hadid and co-founder of dlm Architectural Designers Ltd. He is the author of lectures, exhibitions, workshops and a guest critic at the Yale School of Architecture, ETH Zurich, University of Innsbruck, the Bartlett UCL, Academy of Fine Arts Vienna, Architectural Association London, Swiss Architecture Museum, and many more.

Oliver Domeisen ist ein in London ansässiger Schweizer Architekt, Ornamentalist, Kurator und Akademiker. Er ist Dozent für Geschichte & Theorie an der UCL Bartlett, war Gastdozent am Institut für Experimentelle Architektur der Universität Innsbruck, Gastprofessor an der Akademie der bildenden Künste in Wien, von 2001 bis 2013 Unit Master und von 2013 bis 2017 im Verwaltungsrat an der Architectural Association in London. Zuvor war er tätig als Kurator für zeitgenössische Architektur und Städtebau am V&A Museum, als Projektarchitekt für Zaha Hadid und ist Mitbegründer von dlm architectural designers Ltd. Vorträge, Ausstellungen, Workshops und Gastkritiken an der Yale School of Architecture, ETH Zürich, Universität Innsbruck, The Bartlett UCL, Akademie der bildenden Künste Wien, Architectural Association London, am Schweizerischen Architekturmuseum uvm.

HTK

HYPO Tirol Bank

2020

Bank branch

Kufstein Austria

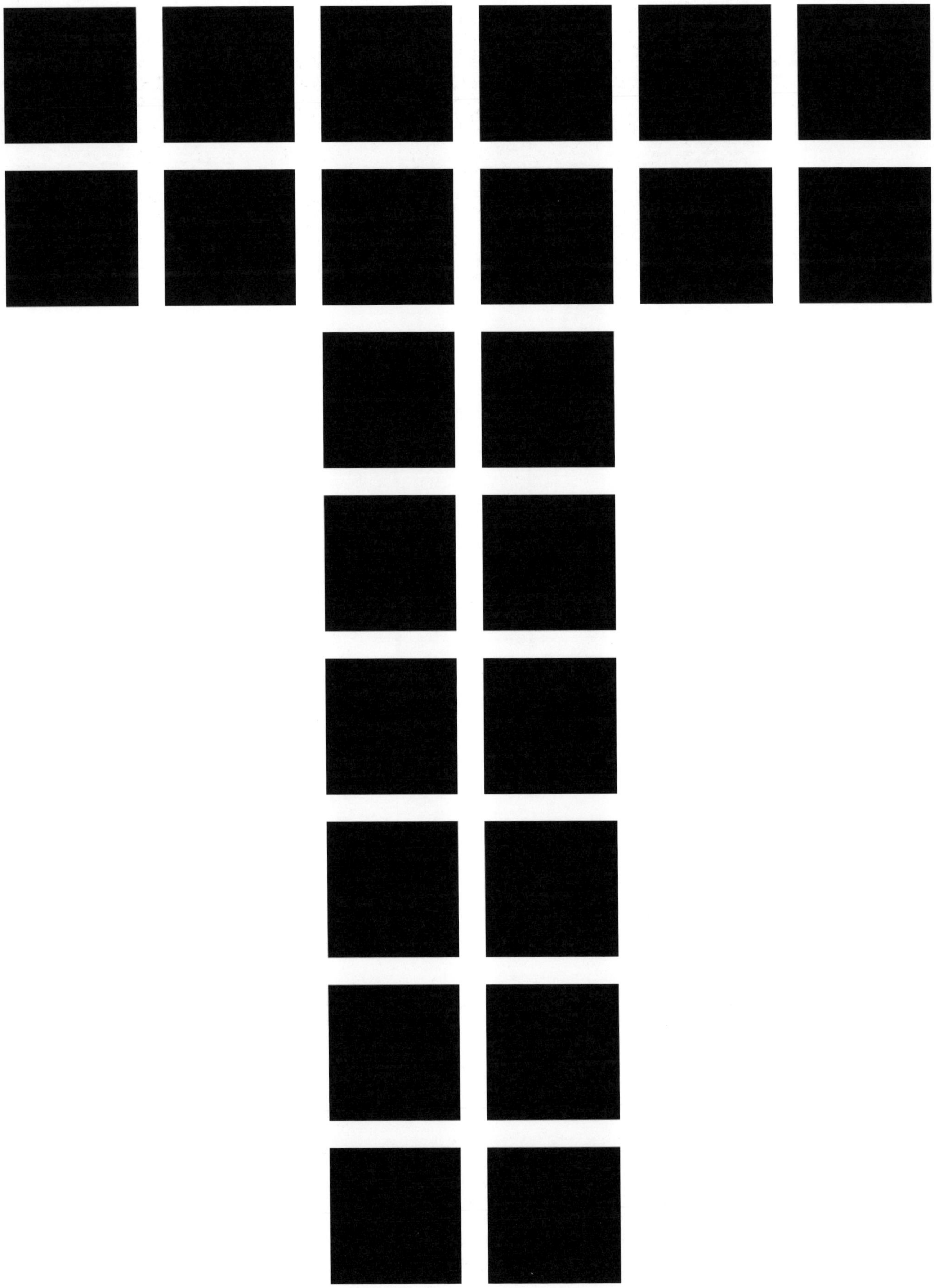

PROJECT TITLE YEAR SUBJECT LOCATION

The design of the Kufstein branch of the Hypo Tirol Bank uses the geometrical recesses of the ostensibly postmodern architecture of the existing building as a means of generating vertically and horizontally interwoven open spaces that communicate with the public realm. Triangles, circles, cubes, volumes and planes articulate and organise the interior as a space that is as welcoming to customers as it is popular amongst employees.

Die Gestaltung der Filiale der Hypo Tirol Bank in Kufstein nützt die geometrischen Einschnitte der postmodern anmutenden Architektur des Bestandsgebäudes, um vertikal und horizontal verschränkte offenen Räume zu erzeugen, die mit dem Stadtraum kommunizieren. Dreieck, Kreis, Kubus und Quader, Volumen und Scheiben formulieren und gliedern den Innenraum kundenorientiert und mitarbeiterfreundlich.

RWI
REAL WEST IMMOBILIEN
bank 99

HYPO TIROL
FEUCHT
ARKADENPLATZ

Thierberg

Spatial concept diagram

Diagramm Raumkonzept

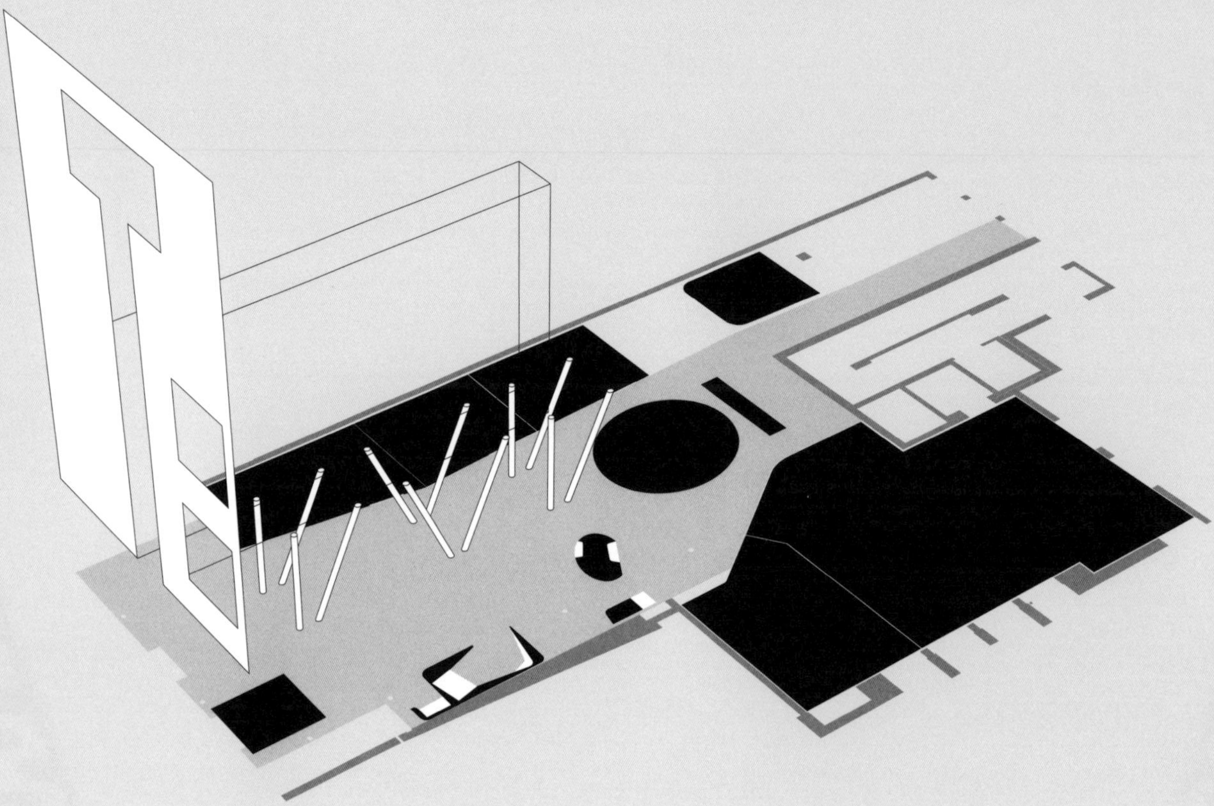

HTS	Hitt und Söhne Bar & Shop	2015	Interior design	Innsbruck Austria
PROJECT	TITLE	YEAR	SUBJECT	LOCATION

The tension between the city and the surrounding mountains is omnipresent in Innsbruck but it is rare to find two architectural icons in close proximity. The café and concept store are located at exactly the point at which the city frees itself from the mountainsides and Franz Baumann's Nordkettenbahn architecture encounters Zaha Hadid's Hungerburgbahn stations, triggering a wonderful dialogue between Tyrolean modernism and the parametric avant-garde. The café takes up this dialogue and positions itself in this context as a sensitive intermediary, without forgetting its own roots in the material and design aesthetic of the 1960s.

Die Spannung zwischen Berg und Stadt ist in Innsbruck allgegenwärtig, die Nachbarschaft zweier Architekturikonen eine Seltenheit. Das Café mit Concept Store befindet sich genau an jener Schnittstelle, an der die Stadt die Berghänge loslässt, die Architektur der Nordkettenbahn von Franz Baumann an die Stationen der Hungerburgbahn von Zaha Hadid anknüpft und damit die Tiroler Moderne mit der parametrischen Avantgarde einen wunderbaren Dialog führt. Das Café nimmt diesen Dialog auf, positioniert sich im Kontext vermittelnd und feinfühlig, ohne dabei die eigene Herkunft aus den 1960er-Jahren und deren Material- und Designästhetik zu vergessen.

TICKETS

black crows
black crows
black crows
SCOTT
MAVE RICK

The bar is a particularly successful and characteristic example of the architecture of the 1950s in Tyrol and is one of the few provable works of the architect Manfred Prachensky.

Das Lokal ist ein besonders gelungenes und charakteristisches Beispiel für die Architektur der 1950er-Jahre in Tirol und eines der wenigen nachweisbaren Werke des Architekten Manfred Prachensky.

TICKETS

CAM	Marktbar and Marktbar Studios	2022	Bar and hotel	Innsbruck Austria
PROJECT	TITLE	YEAR	SUBJECT	LOCATION

The design of the Marktbar in Innsbruck is based on its gastronomic concept, which primarily seeks to attract visitors to the market hall with a range of small, fresh dishes made with interesting produce. The architectural solution pursues a pluralist approach, in which a wide range of materials, forms, colours and patterns are assembled together in a surprising way. This approach is particularly apparent in the treatment of the existing ceiling, which switches from a vault to a flat ceiling with downstand beams, the design of the bar, which combines stainless steel with wood, and the floor, which questions the notion of the homogeneity of the ground in a manner reminiscent of Carlo Scarpa. The design of the hotel rooms also responds to the concept for the Marktbar, while translating this into a more private situation.

Das gastronomische Konzept der Marktbar in Innsbruck, das im Kontext der Markthalle vor allem durch das Angebot kleiner frischer Gerichte mit interessanten Produkten überzeugen soll, ist grundlegend für das Gestaltungskonzept. Die Architektur verfolgt dabei einen pluralistischen Ansatz, der assemblagenhaft verschiedenste Materialien, Formen, Farben und Muster in überraschender Weise verbinden soll. Dieser Ansatz zeigt sich in der Beschaffenheit der Bestandsdecke, die von einem Gewölbe in eine gerade Decke mit Unterzügen wechselt, über die Bar, die Edelstahl und Holz verbindet, bis hin zum Fußboden, der in Reminiszenz an Carlo Scarpa die Idee der Homogenität des Bodens infrage stellt. Ebenso entspricht die Gestaltung der Hotelzimmer dem Entwurfskonzept der Marktbar und übersetzt dieses in eine privatere Situation.

HOT
DRINKS

zu
Vino
SAG ICH
nie no
MARKTBAR

5
2

8

Stefan Marx
And Suddenly It's Morning,
2010, Mural Marktbar.

ARKTBAR
TBAR

PROJECT	TITLE	YEAR	SUBJECT	LOCATION
HGS	Heiliggeist-straße	2021	Residential housing	Innsbruck Austria

The facade of the late-nineteenth-century perimeter block is characterised by openings with varying degrees of decoration. The new corner building in central Innsbruck seeks to reverse the architectural approach of its neighbour by structuring its facade not as a series of openings in a solid wall but as a largely transparent building envelope formed of parapets and an alternating sequence of balconies and opaque elements. In this way, the intermittent structure of the late-nineteenth-century perforated facade is reinterpreted and functionally inverted through the specific use of materials. This rhythmic interplay between glazed and opaque metal elements has a novel but in no way alien impact upon the neighbouring context.

Die Fassade des gründerzeitlichen Blockrands wird geprägt durch mehr oder weniger künstlerisch gestaltete Lochfassaden. Das Eckgebäude in der Innsbrucker Innenstadt versucht einen architektonischen Umkehrschluss, indem es die Fassade nicht durch Öffnungen in einer massiven Wand, sondern durch Brüstungen, alternierende Balkone und blickdichte Elemente in einer größtenteils transparenten Gebäudehülle gliedert. Die punktuelle Gliederung der gründerzeitlichen Lochfassade wird dabei materialspezifisch neu interpretiert und funktional umgekehrt. Das rhythmisierende Wechselspiel von transparenten Glas- und opaken Metallelementen wirkt anders, aber keineswegs fremd im Kontext seiner Nachbarschaft.

The facade is the building's dress, a scaled robe that envelops the body and has pockets to sit in.

Die Fassade ist das Gewand des Gebäudes, ein skaliertes Kleid, das den Körper umhüllt und Taschen hat, um sich hineinzusetzen.

3

BBG	Haus H	2018	Private residence	Innsbruck Austria

PROJECT	TITLE	YEAR	SUBJECT	LOCATION

The house is located in one of the oldest and historically most significant alleys in Innsbruck's St. Nikolaus district. The steep slope and the rural typology of its buildings, the materiality and the atmosphere are typical of the area, as a result of which it unsurprisingly forms part of the protected zone.

In order to ensure the precision of the design and reveal significant features of the existing building, this was measured with a terrestrial laser scanner. Thanks to the scan it was possible to use the special morphology of the historical building, with all its geometrical deviations, imprecisions, recesses and angles, as the basis for the design of an aesthetically powerful contemporary translation.

Das Haus befindet sich in einer der ältesten und historisch bedeutsamsten Gassen im Innsbrucker Stadtteil St. Nikolaus. Durch ihre starke Neigung, die dörfliche Typologie der angrenzenden Gebäude, ihre Materialität und Atmosphäre ist sie für den Stadtteil charakteristisch und dementsprechend Teil der Schutzzone.

Um einen präzisen Entwurf zu erzielen, wurde das Bestandsgebäude mit einem terrestrischen Laserscanner vermessen, der signifikante Merkmale offenbarte. Basierend auf dem Scan, konnten die besondere Morphologie des Altbaus, die geometrischen Abweichungen, Ungenauigkeiten, Einschnitte und Kanten für den Entwurf einer zeitgemäßen Übersetzung gestalterisch wirksam werden.

The historical is an important reference and partner, not to replicate but to find.

Das Historische ist eine wichtige Referenz und ein wichtiger Partner, nicht um nachzuahmen, sondern um zu finden.

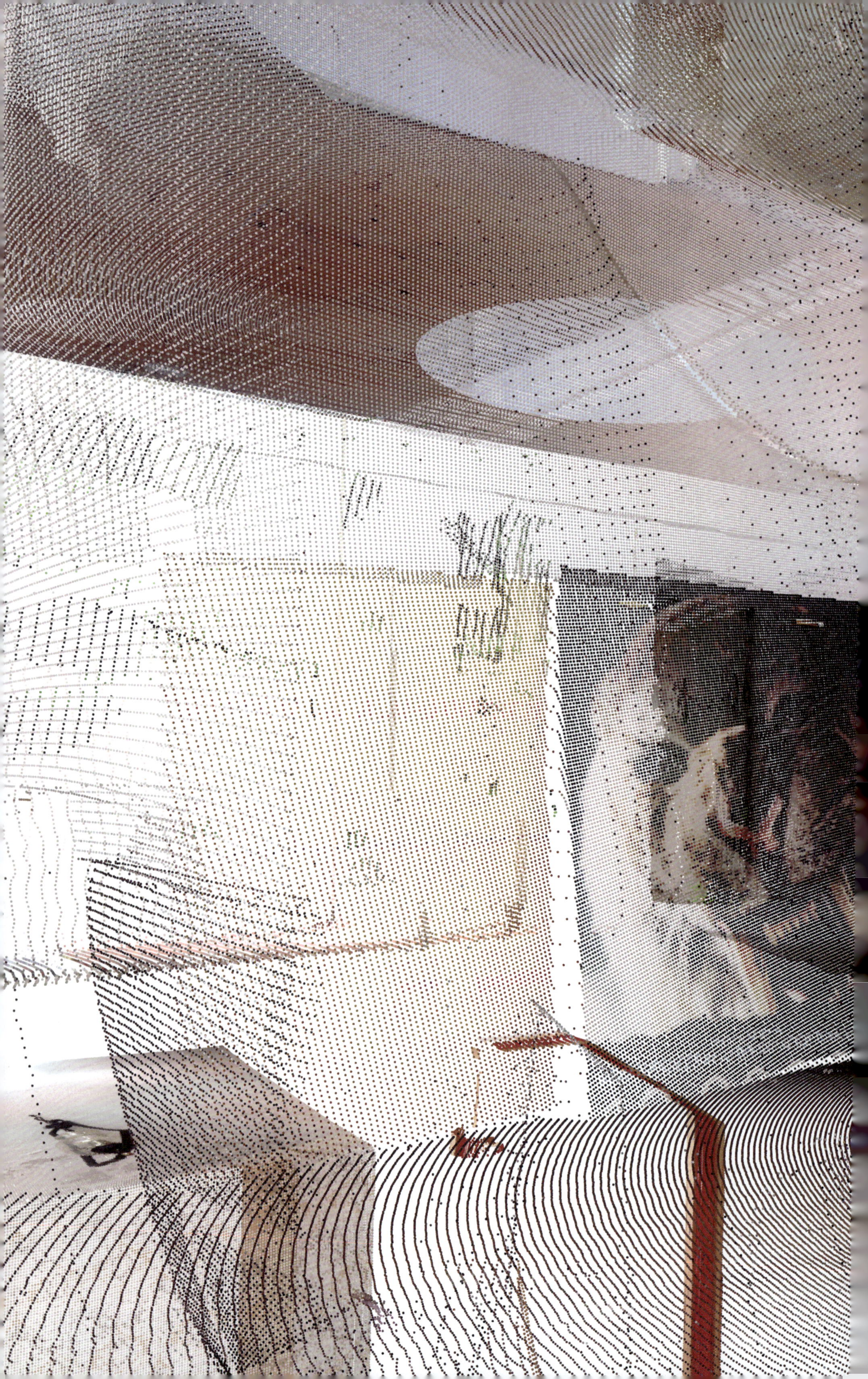

LAAC

The architectural office LAAC, which was founded by Kathrin Aste and Frank Ludin, has been developing and researching innovative answers to urban and landscape challenges for more than fifteen years, together with a network of partners and experts from a range of disciplines. For LAAC, architectural space is engaged in a constant dialogue with its environment. On the basis of this context-oriented understanding of architecture, LAAC strives to establish relationships between place and identity, form and materiality. As a result, architecture is understood as the outcome of processes and as a register of relationships.

As members of the first generation of architects whose training was strongly shaped by digital possibilities, both Kathrin Aste and Frank Ludin regard the potential of the digital and its significance for the creation of place and space as the methodological basis for their design practice.

LAAC understands architectural design as a complex and heteronomous aesthetic practice with the help of which a discourse can be constructed or deconstructed. In this context the design process is not bound to a linear sequence but, rather, can develop in many directions. The common feature of all the projects of LAAC is an enthusiastic treatment of architecture as a landscape with an artistic character and socio-political relevance.

Das Architekturbüro LAAC, gegründet von Kathrin Aste und Frank Ludin, entwickelt und erforscht seit mehr als 15 Jahren, gemeinsam mit einem Netzwerk von Partner*innen und Expert*innen aus verschiedenen Disziplinen, innovative Antworten auf urbane und landschaftliche Herausforderungen. Für LAAC steht der architektonische Raum immer im Austausch und im Kontext mit seiner Umwelt. Mit diesem kontextorientierten Verständnis von Architektur ist LAAC bestrebt, Ort und Identität sowie Form und Materialität in Relation zu bringen. Architektur wird dabei als Resultat von Prozessen und als Verzeichnis von Beziehungen verstanden.

Als erste Generation von Architekt*innen, deren Ausbildung stark durch digitale Möglichkeiten geprägt wurde, ist für beide das Potenzial des Digitalen und dessen Bedeutung für die Genese von Ort und Raum methodische Basis für die Entwurfspraxis. LAAC verstehen den architektonischen Entwurf als eine komplexe und heteronome ästhetische Praxis, mit deren Hilfe ein Diskurs konstruiert oder dekonstruiert werden kann. Dabei ist der Entwurfsprozess nicht an eine lineare Abfolge gebunden, vielmehr kann er sich in viele Richtungen entfalten. Was alle Projekte von LAAC verbindet, ist ein freudiges Verhandeln der Architektur als Landschaft mit einer künstlerischen Beschaffenheit und einer gesellschaftspolitischen Relevanz.

Kathrin Aste

is an Austrian architect, researcher and lecturer. Aste studied architecture at the University of Innsbruck, where she taught at various institutes from 2000 to 2011. From 2011 to 2015 she was a visiting professor at the University of Liechtenstein, from 2014 to 2018 she led the Geography, Landscape and City platform at the Institute of Art and Architecture at the Academy of Fine Arts in Vienna, and in 2015 she was a visiting professor at the Academy of Applied Arts in Vienna. Since 2018 she has headed the unit ./studio3, at the Institute for Experimental Architecture at the University of Innsbruck.

In 2004 she founded the office astearchitecture and since 2009 she has been leading the office LAAC together with Frank Ludin. From 2013 to 2019 she was chairwoman of aut: architektur und tirol.

ist eine österreichische Architektin, Forscherin und Universitätsprofessorin. Sie studierte Architektur an der Universität Innsbruck, wo sie von 2000 bis 2011 an verschiedenen Instituten lehrte. Von 2011 bis 2015 war sie Gastprofessorin an der Universität Liechtenstein, von 2014 bis 2018 leitete sie die Plattform Geografie, Landschaft und Stadt am Institut für Kunst und Architektur an der Akademie der Bildenden Künste in Wien und 2015 war sie Gastprofessorin an der Akademie für Angewandte Kunst in Wien. Seit 2018 leitet sie die Plattform ./studio3, des Instituts für Experimentelle Architektur an der Universität Innsbruck.

2004 gründete sie das Büro astearchitecture und seit 2009 leitet sie es gemeinsam mit Frank Ludin das Büro LAAC. Von 2013 bis 2019 war sie Vorsitzende von aut: architektur und tirol.

Frank Ludin

is an Austrian architect and lecturer. He studied architecture at the University of Innsbruck and taught at the Institute for Experimental Architecture.hochbau from 2004 to 2012. Since 2019 he has been a lecturer at the University of Linz, where he teaches the course überholz – Holzbaukultur. Since 2009 he has been running the office LAAC together with Kathrin Aste and her associated partner Daniel Luckeneder.

ist ein österreichischer Architekt und Lehrbeauftragter. Er studierte Architektur an der Universität Innsbruck und lehrte dort von 2004 bis 2012 am Institut für Experimentelle Architektur.hochbau. Seit 2019 ist er Lehrbeauftragter an der Universität Linz, wo er die Lehrveranstaltung „überholz – Holzbaukultur" unterrichtet. Seit 2009 führt er gemeinsam mit Kathrin Aste und seit 2020 mit ihrem assoziierten Partner Daniel Luckeneder das Büro LAAC.

Daniel Luckenender

is an Austrian architect and lecturer. He studied architecture at the University of Innsbruck and taught at the Institute for Experimental Architecture.hochbau from 2008 to 2013. In 2015 he was a lecturer at ./studio3 at the University of Innsbruck. Since 2018 he leads the office LAAC together with Kathrin Aste and Frank Ludin as an associated partner.

ist ein österreichischer Architekt und Lehrbeauftragter. Er studierte Architektur an der Universität Innsbruck und lehrte dort von 2008 bis 2013 am Institut für Experimentelle Architektur.hochbau. Im Jahr 2015 war er Lehrbeauftragter am ./studio3 der Universität Innsbruck. Seit 2018 führt er das Büro LAAC gemeinsam mit Kathrin Aste und Frank Ludin als assoziierter Partner.

Thanks to all the wonderful people who have ever been a part of LAAC / Danke an alle wunderbaren Menschen die jemals Teil von LAAC waren:

Peter Massin 2007-2022,
Simone Brandstätter 2014-2023,
Benjamin Jenewein 2013-2022,
Teresa Stillebacher 2009-2018,
Simon Benedikt 2014-2022,
Tobias Dorsch 2017-2023,
Felix Steinbacher 2017-2023,
Marc Eduard Ihle 2009-2015,
Ufuk Sagir 2015-2020,
Benjamin Ennemoser 2011-2016,
Julian Fahrenkamp 2018-2023,
Thomas Feuerstein 2007-2011,
Ole Klingemann 2014-2017,
Simon Paukner 2019-2022,
Laura Winterberg 2020-2022,
Pia Grobner 2016-2018,
Patrizia Pfanzelt 2015-2017,
Allison Weiler 2012-2014,
Valentine Troi 2007-2009,
Alexander Mühlauer 2007-2009,
Luis Navarro 2020-2021,
Oliver Hamedinger 2020-2021,
Fabian Teufel 2020-2021,
Fabien Stoque 2015-2016,
Serdar Oeztuerk 2014-2015,
Alexander Neuwirth 2015-2016,
Alexander Beck 2015-2016,
Rupert Maleczek 2014-2015,
Thomas Pukljak 2014-2015,
Clara Jaschke 2012-2013,
Phillipe Grotenrath 2011-2012,
Ferdinand Fritz 2009-2010,
Paul Böhm 2020,
Raffael Schwärzler 2019,
Cenk Güzelis 2016,
Lino Lanzmaier 2016,
Spela Leskovic 2015,
Courtney Jones 2015,
Moritz Hanshans 2015,
Elke Heidegger 2015,
Sophia Spiss 2014,
David Stieler 2014,
Julia Gottstein 2013,
Thomas Tait 2013,
Ivan Niedermair 2013,
Alexander Topf 2013,
Phillip Zimmermann 2013,
David Fischer 2010,
Barbara Jeller 2010,
Sylvia Naschberger 2010,
Andreas Hörl 2007.

TOP

Top of Tyrol
Stubai Glacier, Austria, 2008
Viewing platform
Client: Wintersport Tirol AG
Project partner: aste weissteiner zt-gmbh
Team: Kathrin Aste, Thomas Feuerstein, Frank Ludin
→ 33

NPO

Nature on Stage
Ötztal Nature Park, Austria, 2015
Client: Naturpark Ötztal
Project partner: Liquid Frontiers
Team: Kathrin Aste, Benjamin Ennemoser, Marc Ihle, Daniel Luckeneder, Frank Ludin, Peter Massin
→ 45

SDI

Sustainable Design for Alpine Infrastructures
Research project, 2012
Project partner: alpS GmbH
Team: Kathrin Aste, Benjamin Ennemoser, Marc Ihle, Clara Jaschke, Daniel Luckeneder, Frank Ludin, Peter Massin, Allison Weiler
→ 67

CCN

Copa Cagrana
Donauplatte Vienna, Austria, 2021
Urban beach
Client: Wiener Gewässer Management GmbH
Project partner: Darko Stevanovic
Team: Kathrin Aste, Simon Benedikt, Benjamin Ennemoser, Pia Grobner, Ole Klingemann, Frank Ludin, Patrizia Pflanzelt, Ufuk Sagir, Felix Steinbacher, Fabien Stoque
→ 77

VAB

Sphäre 1:50.000
Exhibition: Austrian Pavilion Venice Architecture Biennale 2018
Commissioner / Curator: Verena Konrad
Team: Kathrin Aste, Simon Benedikt, Simone Brandstätter, Julian Fahrenkamp, Daniel Luckeneder, Frank Ludin, Teresa Stillebacher
Construction team: Jakob Breitenlechner, Michael Gassebner, Raphael Hanny, Hannes Höck, Lino Lanzmaier, Thomas Obererlacher, Ufuk Sagir, Matthias Trobos
Further exhibitors: Henke Schreieck Architekten, Sagmeister&Walsh
→ 103

LHP

Landhausplatz
Innsbruck, Austria, 2010
Public square
Client: Amt der Tiroler Landesregierung
Project partners: Stiefel Kramer Architecture, Christopher Grüner
Team: Kathrin Aste, Thomas Feuerstein, Frank Ludin, Peter Massin
→ 115

PMA

P2 Urban Hybrid
Innsbruck, Austria, 2018
Residential building and public space
Client: Pema Group
Team: Kathrin Aste, Simon Benedikt, Simone Brandstätter, Marc Ihle, Benjamin Jenewein, Daniel Luckeneder, Frank Ludin, Rupert Maleczek, Peter Massin, Ivan Niedermair, Ufuk Sagir, Allison Weiler, Phillip Zimmermann
→ 163

SBI

City Library
Innsbruck, Austria, 2018
Library
Client: Stadt Innsbruck
Project partner: Liquid Frontiers
Art: Trurl by Thomas Feuerstein
Team: Kathrin Aste, Simon Benedikt, Simone Brandstätter, Benjamin Jenewein, Daniel Luckeneder, Frank Ludin, Ufuk Sagir
→ 177

MPV
MPREIS Volders
Volders, Austria, 2022
Supermarket and housing
Client: MPREIS Warenvertriebs GmbH
Team: Kathrin Aste, Simon Benedikt, Simone Brandstätter, Julian Fahrenkamp, Daniel Luckeneder, Frank Ludin, Simon Paukner, Laura Winterberg
→ 197

MPW
MPREIS Weer
Weer, Austria, 2017
Supermarket
Client: MPREIS Warenvertriebs GmbH
Team: Kathrin Aste, Simon Benedikt, Simone Brandstätter, Ole Klingemann, Daniel Luckeneder, Frank Ludin, Ufuk Sagir
→ 209

MPS
MPREIS Sölden
Sölden, Austria, 2022
Supermarket
Client: MPREIS Warenvertriebs GmbH
Team: Kathrin Aste, Simon Benedikt, Simone Brandstätter, Tobias Dorsch, Julian Fahrenkamp, Daniel Luckeneder, Frank Ludin, Peter Massin
→ 221

HTK
HYPO Tirol
Kufstein, Austria, 2020
Conversion office and residential building
Client: Hypo Tirol Bank
Team: Kathrin Aste, Simon Benedikt, Benjamin Jenewein, Daniel Luckeneder, Frank Ludin, Felix Steinbacher
→ 239

HTS
Hitt und Söhne
Innsbruck, Austria, 2015
Bar
Client: Schorsch Gastronomie GmbH, Margit Mölk-Kröll
Team: Kathrin Aste, Alexander Beck, Simone Brandstätter, Benjamin Ennemoser, Benjamin Jenewein, Spela Leskovic, Daniel Luckeneder, Frank Ludin, Serdar Ötztürk, Ufuk Sagir
→ 251

CAM
Marktbar and Marktbar Studios
Innsbruck, Austria, 2022
Bar and hotel
Client: Stephanie Cammerlander
Team: Kathrin Aste, Tobias Dorsch, Julian Fahrenkamp, Daniel Luckeneder, Frank Ludin, Simon Paukner, Fabian Teufel, Laura Winterberg
→ 263

HGS
Urban Living
Innsbruck, Austria, 2021
Residential building
Client: MOSER Wohnbau & Immobilien GmbH
Team: Kathrin Aste, Tobias Dorsch, Julian Fahrenkamp, Benjamin Jenewein, Daniel Luckeneder, Frank Ludin, Ufuk Sagir
→ 277

BBG
Haus H
Innsbruck, Austria, 2022
Private residence
Client: Private
Project partner: Nina Mair Architecture + Design
Team: Kathrin Aste, Simone Brandstätter, Daniel Luckeneder, Frank Ludin, Peter Massin, Simon Paukner, Raffael Schwärzler, Felix Steinbacher
→ 287

Editors / Herausgeber*innen:
LAAC, Kathrin Aste & Frank Ludin
Texts / Texte:
Kathrin Aste, Roger Connah,
Oliver Domeisen, Frank Ludin,
Claudia Pasquero, Marco Russo,
Florian Waldvogel
Translations / Übersetzungen:
Rupert Hebblethwaite, Karlheinz
Rathgeb-Weber
Copy-editing / Lektorat:
Park Books, Astrid Flögel
Proofreading / Korrektorat:
Miriam Seifert-Waibel
Design / Gestaltung:
CIRCUS. Büro für Kommunikation
und Gestaltung
Unter Mitarbeit von /
With the collaboration of:
Kathrin Aste and / und Simone
Brandstätter
Printing and binding /
Druck und Bindung:
Druckerei Gugler
Paper / Papier:
Fedrigoni, Ispira, Biancho
Purezza, 360 g/m²; Fedrigoni,
Arena, Extrawhite rough 120 g/m²
Font / Schrift:
ABC Diatype, ABC Diatype Mono

Image credits / Bildnachweis:
Günther Egger (239, 242-243, 244, 245, 247, 248-249, 263, 266-267, 269, 270, 273)
Martin Fehrer (88, 89)
Thomas Feuerstein (178)
Jenny Haimerl (268, 271)
Kingpin (123)
LAAC mit Artfabrik (92-93, 95, 99, 100-101)
LAAC mit Cenk Güzelis (52-53)
LAAC Pointcloud (288-289, 296-297)
Marc Lins Photography (10-11, 12-13, 16-17, 20-21, 77, 80-81, 90-91, 103, 110, 111, 112, 113, 163, 166-167, 168-169, 174-175, 177, 180-181, 184, 185, 186, 188, 189, 190-191, 192, 193, 200-201, 202, 203, 204, 205, 206-207, 212-213, 214, 215, 218, 219, 221, 224-225, 226, 227, 228, 229, 274-275, 277, 280-281, 282, 283, 284, 285, 287, 290-291, 292, 293, 294-295)
Frank Ludin (8-9, 33, 34-35, 36-37, 39, 41, 43)
Guy Marjus (78-79)
Stefan Marx (272)
Martin Mischkulnig (107, 108-109)
Harry Putz (42)
Lukas Schaller (18-19, 209, 251, 254-255, 256, 257, 259, 260-261)
Christoph Schwarz (156-157, 158-159)
Günter Richard Wett (14-15, 45, 48-49, 54, 56, 57, 115, 118-119, 121, 124-125, 126, 127, 128-129, 130, 131, 134-135, 136-137, 138-139)

Published by / Erschienen bei:
Park Books
Niederdorfstrasse 54
8001 Zürich
Schweiz / Switzerland
www.park-books.com

Edition / Auflage:
1st edition, 500 copies /
1. Auflage, 500 Stück

Printed in / Gedruckt in:
Austria / Österreich

Park Books is being supported by the Federal Office of Culture with a general subsidy for the years 2021-2024.

Park Books wird vom Bundesamt für Kultur mit einem Strukturbeitrag für die Jahre 2021-2024 unterstützt.

ISBN 978-3-03860-327-6

Special thanks to / Besonderer Dank geht an:
Christian Aste, Martin Baldauf, Jörg Büchlmann, Volker Giencke, Sabine Dreher, Hugo Dworzak, Armin Ennemoser, Claudia and / und Günter Höfert, Reinhard Klier, Verena Konrad, Rainer Köberl, Margit Kröll-Mölk, Hansjörg Mölk, Arno Ritter, Hanno Schlögl, Hannes Stiefel, Christian Switak, Kjetil Thorsen, Wolfgang Tschapeller, Florian Waldvogel and / und Clara, Hanna, Jakob, Mara, Mia, Petra and / und Stephanie.